asian cook

Terry Tan

photography by Michael Paul

asian cook

METRO BOOKS
NEW YORK

This book is dedicated to my son,
Christopher Tan, who has done me proud
by following in my footsteps by becoming
a food writer, chef, and serious foodie.

Publisher Jacqui Small
Art Director Valerie Fong
Tools photography Nat Rea
Food Styling Terry Tan, Kit Chan, Emi Kazuko
Project Editor Jenni Muir
Copy Editor Marion Moisy
Production Geoff Barlow
American adaptation American Pie, London and Sunnyvale

Metro Books
122 Fifth Avenue
New York, NY 10011

ISBN: 978-1-4351-2546-9

Printed and bound in Singapore

10 9 8 7 6 5 4 3 2 1

RECIPE NOTES: Oils All recipes require the use of a light oil with a neutral
taste, such as corn, sunflower, grapeseed, safflower, or peanut oil. Use olive oil only
where specified. **Eggs** are large. **Sugar** is granulated white or superfine sugar
unless otherwise specified. **Pepper** is freshly ground black pepper unless otherwise specified. **Spoon and cup measurements** Use only standard
measuring spoons and cups. Table flatware and hollowware vary in capacity.
Spoon measurements are level. **Preparation time** includes cooking time;
soaking or marinating times are given separately.

contents

introduction

Most people in the West believe that Asian kitchens are exotic— full of strange and rustic implements, of granite mortars that need forklifts to move them and cast-iron woks that rust before you can say "stir-fry." True, some tools used in Asian cooking can seem esoteric, even mystifying, but most are very simple to use. Take the granite mortar and pestle: It has been around for centuries and is small and light enough for even a child to use. I inherited mine from my grandmother, which makes it older than I am! It has now worn to a silky smoothness and grinds spices and aromatics beautifully into emulsion-like pastes.

It is fascinating and therapeutic to grind, grate, slice, and chop using age-old tools and implements. They seem to impart an extra and mysterious dimension of flavor to the dish cooked, and, despite the introduction of food processors, true quality and authenticity for many dishes are often only achievable by using traditional tools that have stood the test of time. Most are easy to use, and few require painstaking instructions; however, frequent practice helps produce perfect results. In the pantheon of good, authentic cooking, there is much to be said for using implements designed for specific tasks. Even better, they make wonderful heirlooms to hand down to the next generation.

For generations, Asians have used a wide range of the tools chronicled in this book. Some implements have been threatened with extinction, but more than a few have been saved from the back burner of history, modernized, and even adapted into exciting new electrical appliances. Much of what can be found in Asian kitchens is available in specialty stores and ethnic supermarkets, many of which now have their own web sites. Some tools may be harder to track down, but most avid cooks agree this is all part of the fun of exploring the cuisines of other lands.

Geographically, the Asia we refer to here embraces China; India, Pakistan, and Sri Lanka; Japan and Korea; the five distinct countries of Myanmar (formerly Burma), Laos, Kampuchea (formerly Cambodia), Thailand, and Vietnam; and the spice islands of the Indonesian archipelago and neighboring Malaysia and Singapore, collectively known as Southeast Asia. Although Laotian and Kampuchean cooking are relatively unknown in the Western world, they share common characteristics with their neighboring countries.

Even though contemporary lifestyles dictate the need for high-tech appliances, Asian kitchens still contain tools evocative of the agrarian way of life. There is a special relationship between their aesthetic and their functionality. For instance, banana leaf serves as a mat for steamed coconut rice while imparting a distinctive fragrance to the dish. When Thai sticky rice is served in a woven banana-leaf basket, the flavor is subtly enhanced.

High-tech appliances may well make short work of food processing, but speed is not the be-all and end-all of kitchen craft. The true enjoyment of food often dictates that some effort must be made. The split-second timing of stir-frying, the consistency and delicacy of dumpling dough, and the smoothness of spice pastes are all dependent on using the correct tool. Even the simplest items can be used ingeniously. Two-foot-long chopsticks are a good example. When you deep-fry food, if you pick up the cooked morsels using a conventional ladle or tongs, you run the risk of hot fat splattering on you. With very long chopsticks, the distance between cook and wok ensures that there is no danger.

Several of the tools and foods featured in this book have traditional symbolic, religious, or mystical significance, and it can only enhance your enjoyment to dwell a little on the hidden symbolism. Every Japanese dish reflects a mood dictated by a season, whereas the Chinese love roundness because it symbolizes eternity. Whatever your reason for exploring the East, be it buying a wok, re-creating food sampled on vacation, or looking for an exciting wrap for dumplings, I hope you enjoy using this book and the tools featured in it.

material choice

This list explains the pros and cons of the principal materials from which the eclectic range of Asian cooking equipment is made or naturally derived. It also provides guidance on care, preparation, cleaning, and storage of your tools.

aluminum

Uses Pots, steamers, tiffin carriers, storage tins, cake molds, ladles, and woks.
Pros Cheap, lightweight, and conducts heat well and evenly, as long as the gauge is heavy enough.
Cons Reacts with acidic elements in food and there-fore will discolor certain foods or impart a metallic taste. The metal tends to discolor and pit. Thin-gauge aluminum warps easily and heats unevenly.
Care Wash in hot soapy water, using a scouring pad if necessary. Remove stains by boiling in a weak solution of vinegar or cream of tartar.

anodized aluminum

Uses As for aluminum.
Pros The electrochemical process gives aluminum a hard, dense oxide coating that resists corrosion. Hard anodizing also changes the molecular structure of the aluminum, making it harder than steel and creating excellent heat distribution.
Cons Dishwasher detergents rub away the coating.
Care Wash in hot soapy water. Do not use scouring pads. To remove burned-on food, fill with a mild solution of vinegar and water and bring to a boil. Anodized aluminum pans can also benefit from a light coating of oil before storage. Maintain color with the manufacturer's proprietary cleaner.

bamboo

Uses Utensils, steamers, lids, and barbecue skewers.
Pros Inexpensive, lightweight, and nonreactive to foods. Its porosity is an advantage for steaming.
Cons Can become brittle with frequent use; relatively short life, will warp and burn if not handled carefully.
Care Wash with hot water only, because the material is porous and absorbs cleaning fluids.

brass

Uses Cake and pastry molds and mortars and pestles.
Pros An alloy of copper and zinc, with other metals such as aluminum and tin added for strength and to prevent corrosion. Brass is tough, corrosion-resistant, and rust-free—functional as well as beautiful.
Cons Can be extremely heavy.
Care Wash with hot soapy water or in detergent.

cast iron

Uses Pots, pans, griddles, grill pans, mortars, Dutch ovens, and teapots.
Pros Durable, strong, does not warp, and conducts heat evenly and retains it well. Great for long, slow cooking using a minimal amount of fat.

Cons Very heavy, so best for a pan that remains fairly static during cooking, such as a Dutch oven. The density makes it slow to heat. If dropped on a hard floor, it may break. If cast iron pots and pans do not have an enamel or nonstick surface they must be seasoned with oil to prevent sticking and rusting.
Care Avoid uncoated cast iron. Wipe with paper towels. Remove stuck-on food by lightly scouring under hot running water. Dry well and coat with oil before storing. Brush the cooking surface with oil before each use, then wipe off before adding oil for cooking. Wash coated cast iron with hot, soapy water but do not scour. To remove stubborn residue from coated cast iron pans, leave them to soak.

ceramics

Uses Dutch oven, herb pots, and mortars and pestles.
Pros Nonreactive and inexpensive. Unglazed earthenware is porous and retains heat and moisture well. Excellent for slow oven cooking or in a microwave.
Cons Brittle and can break if there are sudden or extreme temperature changes. Generally not flame-resistant, though good quality ceramic pots can be used on a heat diffuser over a low flame.
Care Wash glazed or partially glazed pots in hot, soapy water, without scouring. Completely unglazed pots should be scrubbed clean in salt water. Do not use detergent because this taints the food.

clay and terra-cotta

Uses Clay (or "sand") pots, mortars, and yogurt pots.
Pros Attractive, rustic, nonreactive. Wire mesh support is used to protect oven-to-table ware from damage.
Cons Cracks easily if roughly handled. Clay pots do not take well to direct flame cooking.
Care Wash and dry, but never use detergents because the material is absorbent. Dishwasher safe. Never store them stacked one in another, because this will cause cracking.

coconut shell

Uses The outer hard casing of the coconut is shaped into all sorts of implements, including bowls, ladles, serving utensils, spoons, and spatulas.
Pros Nonreactive, inexpensive, rustic, versatile.
Cons Can be hard to find in the West, and few matching sets are available. Cracks easily, and some discoloration can occur when used for spices.
Care Wash in hot soapy water. To remove stuck-on food, scrub or scour, but not with detergents.

copper

Uses Karahis, molds, and wire-mesh ladles.
Pros First choice of Western chefs for saucepans; used less frequently in Asia because of high cost. Some Asian pots and pans may be lightly copper-plated, but copper mainly used as mesh. It does not rust or become brittle.
Cons Expensive and needs careful handling. Reacts with acids and discolors easily.

Care Wash in hot, soapy water. Never use scouring pads. To bring up the shine, soak copper pans and utensils in a little vinegar and dry with a soft cloth.

granite
Uses An ancient material used mainly in heavy grinding tools, and for some serving dishes.
Pros Virtually indestructible, but will break if dropped from a height. Stainless, nontoxic, and nonreactive.
Cons Heavy, clumsy to use, and difficult to clean.
Care Wash with hot water and a mild detergent. Scrub with a steel wool pad after grinding spices, and soak in hot water to remove strong odors.

lacquerware
Uses Bowls, plates, bento boxes, trays, and other serving dishes. Favored in Japan for thousands of years. The sap from the lacquer tree is applied in many layers, then heated and allowed to dry.
Pros Beautiful, lightweight, portable, delicate but tough enough for dishwashers. Retains heat well, does not stain, nontoxic, and nonreactive.
Cons Lacquerware cannot be used for cooking and may chip if knocked or dropped.
Care Wash in hot soapy water and dry with a soft cloth to prevent staining.

leaves, dried
Uses Mainly from bamboo and lotus plants. Dried leaves are used for wrapping and encasing savory and sweet dishes prior to steaming or boiling.
Pros Impart a distinctive fragrance and have a long shelf life if stored properly. Inexpensive and disposable.
Cons Crack and tear easily if not handled gently.
Care Must be kept in a cool, dry place.

leaves, dried baskets
Uses Throughout Asia, dried pandanus (screw pine), coconut, rattan, bamboo, and other broad leaves are woven into fans, baskets, and food containers.
Pros They are relatively inexpensive (except when crafted and sold as exotic and ornamental in gift stores!). Excellent for steam-and-serve dishes. Unless waxed or otherwise treated with a coating, they do not react to cooking agents such as oil and vinegar, except that they may darken after use.
Cons They are not durable, and strips may unravel after a while. They can also lose their shape.
Care Easy to wash and dry but not dishwasher safe because of the delicate weave.

leaves, fresh
Uses Leaves such as banana, pandanus (screw pine), bamboo, and yam are used for wrapping, encasing, and perfuming foods, especially when steaming. Banana leaves are also cut into large pieces and employed as serving plates in tropical parts of Asia.
Pros Although scented, some are not edible, because of their fibrous nature. They are inexpensive and disposable, and provide a natural, authentic presentation.
Cons Fresh leaves are delicate, tear easily, and have a short shelf life. Some are only available fresh in the country in which they are grown.
Care Fresh leaves must be kept wrapped in a cool, dry place for no more than a few days.

porcelain
Uses Plates, bowls, spoons, rice scoops, and tureens.
Pros Can be delicate or tough, depending on manufacture. Chinese and Japanese porcelain have been famous for centuries for their beauty and functionality. Porcelain retains heat well but is cool to the touch; nonporous and nonreactive. Microwave friendly, except for items with a metallic paint finish.
Cons Fragile, should not be used over direct heat, and needs careful cleaning.
Care Wash in hot soapy water. Soak to remove stuck-on food. Porcelain is generally dishwasher safe unless otherwise specified by the manufacturer.

stainless steel
Uses Pots, pans, woks, ladles, scoops, serving dishes, storage containers, knives, and cleavers.
Pros One of the toughest and most enduring materials. Pristine-looking, long-lasting, hygienic, rustproof, and nonreactive. Immune to corrosion and pitting. Made "stainless" by the inclusion of chrome. It also contains nickel, described as 18/10, which means the ratio of chrome to nickel is 18 percent to 10 percent, respectively. The stainless steel used in knives contains a lower percentage of chrome (at least 12 percent) and 0.15–0.8 percent carbon, to provide additional strength. This reduction in chrome makes carbon–steel knives prone to staining.
Cons Stainless steel is a poor and uneven conductor of heat, but the bases of some woks and pots incorporate a layer of aluminum or copper to alleviate this problem. Good stainless steel pots have bases containing at least ⅛ inch of aluminum or ⅙ inch of copper. Stainless steel is not entirely stainless and will discolor or spot if left in contact with hard water, salt water, acidic juices, or even some detergents when not rinsed thoroughly after washing. Small pits may form.
Care Clean with hot soapy water, using a nylon scourer if necessary. Avoid bleach and harsh abrasives. Soak off stuck-on foods, and remove stubborn stains with a proprietary stainless steel cleaner.

wood
Uses Asian woods come in varying degrees of hardness. They are often used for cake molds, trays, bowls, steamer trivets, chopsticks, pot rests and lids, tubs, tongs, and rolling pins.
Pros Beautiful, durable, inexpensive, does not warp or break, natural, and nonreactive to foods.
Cons Can be heavy and is prone to discoloration if used with highly colored ingredients.
Care Wash in hot soapy water, and scrub gently with a soft brush, especially when cleaning cake molds that feature intricately carved designs.

china

china and its regions

"If there be only one note, there can be no music. If there be one flavor, there would be no satisfaction. If sugar is added to vinegar, there would be the universal harmony of sweet and sour." So said Yen Tzu, a disciple of Confucius, circa 600 B.C. This is the philosophy that underscores Chinese cuisine.

China is a vast country with enormous climatic and geographical variations. The cuisine has evolved over more than 3,000 years and developed in an environment of constant change with occasional periods of relative stability. Today, ancient traditions and culinary innovations exist in delicious synergy.

About 80 percent of the 1.6 billion people still live a rural life, engaged in agriculture. Despite a shortage of fertile arable land, Chinese farmers have learned to nourish the soil to produce bountiful harvests. Centuries-old, terraced paddy fields maximize the use of water, even though there are frequent droughts. Despite the advent of refrigeration, Chinese people still insist on the freshest foods available and often shop several times a day to ensure this.

There are distinct regional schools in Chinese cuisine that are roughly delineated by the geographical boundaries of the northern, eastern, southern, and western regions, better known as Beijing, Shanghai, Cantonese, and Sichuan (or Szechuan) cuisine, respectively. Each is steeped in indigenous traditions. There are also lesser known types such as the Muslim school of northeast China, Hunanese, Hainanese (from Hainan Island), and several sub-schools within the southern Chinese province of Guangdong. Hong Kong, though a part of South China, has also evolved its own distinctive style.

The name of China's northern capital city has undergone no less than eight changes since it was first named Chi in 481 B.C. At various stages, throughout the next 2,500 years of political upheaval and other changes, it has been called Yenking, Chungtu, Tatu, and Khanbalyk (under the rule of Kublai Khan), Peking, Peiping, and finally Beijing.

Severe winters, short growing seasons, and an arid climate have created a hearty cuisine. The staples grown throughout the region are wheat, millet, and soybeans. Rice is not suited to the climate and therefore rarely features in northern Chinese meals. The preference is for steamed wheat-flour buns and noodles.

Northern cuisine is regarded as the most sophisticated of all, although it is robust and features simple ingredients. Its chief characteristic is the frequent and lavish use of soybean paste, which is the basis of many well-known sauces, including hoisin and yellow bean. Heavily influenced by the vast hinterland of Mongolia and beyond that, by the sea on its eastern shores, northern Chinese cooking features many lamb and duck dishes, which may be roasted, braised, or barbecued. Peking Duck is regarded as a national treasure.

The Yangtze River, China's longest waterway, leaves its mountain source in the Tibetan Plateau and flows through Sichuan before ending in the East

ABOVE: 1 bean thread noodles, 2 rice noodles, 3 egg noodles, 4 rice, 5 egg dumpling (wonton) wrappers, 6 rice dumpling (wonton) wrappers. OPPOSITE: 1 baby bok choy, 2 mustard greens, 3 snow peas, 4 scallions, 5 bean sprouts.

China Sea, just north of Shanghai. Eastern China is covered by a vast network of lakes and tributaries and is a leading agricultural region, boasting some of the most fertile land in the country. Barley, wheat, rice, corn, sweet potatoes, peanuts, and soybeans grow in abundance here. The region offers diverse cooking styles, but all emphasize freshness and pure, natural flavors. Eastern China's stir-fried dishes are often simple, seasoned only with soy sauce and pepper. Lotus grows profusely in the ponds, lakes, and streams, so many dishes are wrapped in lotus leaves and steamed.

The mountains of the warmer southern reaches of Eastern China feature many tea plantations. Fujian is perhaps the best known of China's tea-growing provinces. Early nineteenth-century trade with Europe in this precious leaf brought prosperity to the local inhabitants, whose leisured classes were

ABOVE: 1 dark soy sauce, 2 oyster sauce, 3 bamboo shoots, 4 salted and fermented black beans, 5 light soy sauce, 6 hoisin sauce, 7 sesame oil, 8 five-spice powder, 9 Sichuan pepper, 10 water chestnuts, 11 white sesame seeds, 12 fresh ginger root, 13 dried shiitake mushrooms.

subsequently able to cultivate a taste for exquisite cooking. Fujian chefs are extremely fond of pork, using all the variety meats in highly imaginative ways, including dishes of steamed pig's blood. The long coastline, rivers, and freshwater lakes are full of the fish and seafood that also typifies this cuisine.

In the West, Sichuan has a tongue-tingling reputation as the fiery cauldron of chili peppers. However chilies are not the be-all and end-all of the region's cooking, and several festive and banquet dishes are completely devoid of fire. The purpose of chili peppers is not, as it sometimes seems, to paralyze the tongue but merely to stimulate the palate, making it more sensitive and receptive to the mul-

tiple flavors. Many of the sauces are a medley of hot, sweet, sour, aromatic, and fragrant flavors, and Sichuanese dishes often break traditional culinary rules to brilliant effect. The range of dishes is delectable, from exquisite jade shrimps and fire-exploded kidney flowers to popular sweet-and-sour pork, aromatic crispy duck, and hot-and-sour soup.

The name Sichuan literally means "Four Rivers," though there are more than twice this number, all tributaries of the mighty Yangtze River. A region of searingly hot summers and mild winters, Sichuan supports an astonishing range of plant foods and a wealth of subtropical fruits, including oranges, limes, apples, plums, and lychees. Sichuan teas are also justly famous, especially those from the West Lake area. The finest variety is Dragon Well tea.

Historically, the southern province of Guangdong was allied to the former Guangxi province, now an autonomous region. Lying in the shadow of the Guangdong–Guangxi Mountains, the region is crisscrossed by three tributaries of the Yangtse, the best-known being the Pearl River that has given its name to soy sauce and other products.

Rice is the staple grain. Peanuts, coconuts, pineapple, sugar cane, tea, and coffee, as well as tobacco and rubber, are grown in abundance. There was much contact with Indian, Persian, and Arab traders before the fifteenth century and after that, Portuguese, British, Dutch, and French merchants visited regularly.

The magic of this region's cooking, usually called Cantonese, is in its texture. Natural flavors are not altered during the cooking process, and preparation is kept to a minimum. Absolute freshness is vital. The aim is to control crispness and subtlety, but perhaps the most distinctive aspect of Cantonese cuisine is its strongly savory flavor. Seafoods are often incorporated into meat cooking, for instance, in the form of oyster and shrimp sauces. Salted and fermented black beans also impart a strong taste, while ginger counteracts any fishiness and garlic provides fragrance.

The former British colony of Hong Kong is a magnet for world travelers and businesspeople, and its cuisine has evolved accordingly. The demand for quality has forced local chefs to strive constantly to achieve excellence and innovation, developing a reputation for cutting-edge cuisine. Today, many Chinese restaurants around the world take pride in promoting "Hong Kong–style" dishes on their menus, meaning Cantonese food with an innovative twist.

cleaver and cutting board

China's characteristic knife, the cleaver, may seem like a lethal guillotine to the uninitiated, but it is surprisingly easy to use. Its versatility as chopper, slicer, crusher, tenderizer, and scoop effectively eliminates the need for a battery of knives in the kitchen. With care, a cleaver can last more than a lifetime, and in China (as well as in the Chinese diaspora countries of Singapore, Indonesia, and Malaysia) the family knife is often passed on to the next generation.

1 Cutting board Chinese people traditionally use a block of natural hardwood, a complete round cut from a whole tree trunk rather than several pieces of wood fused together, as many cutting boards are today. The furious chopping action of the heavy Chinese cleaver will inevitably chip a synthetic board, but a natural wood board can absorb the blows without splintering. Cleaning such boards can be a problem. Chinese chefs use their cleavers to scrape off any embedded bits of food in order to prevent contamination. As a result, over time, the boards become slightly concave.

2, 3, 4 Cleavers Heavier than most other knives, the cleaver is honed to razor sharpness and balanced to give the leverage needed to cut through joints of meat and even bone. There are several sizes and weights made from a variety of materials. Cleavers may have wooden handles or be cast from a single piece of metal. Although the modern stainless steel models produced by Western manufacturers may look impressive, they tend to require frequent sharpening, as do the old-fashioned iron knives sold in Chinese supermarkets. A better choice is carbonized steel, which should be wiped rather than washed after use, to prevent discoloration, and given a light coat of vegetable oil to prevent rusting.

Using a cleaver

Peeling With the fingertips of one hand, hold down the piece of root vegetable firmly. Hold the cleaver in your other hand with its sharp edge between the skin and the flesh. Press down firmly all the way to peel off one strip of skin at a time. Turn the vegetable and repeat until all the skin has been peeled.

Tenderizing meat Turn the cleaver over so that the blunt end is facing downward. Bring the clever down firmly all over the sliced meat, turning the meat over once to beat other side. When properly tenderized, the meat should have slight grooves in it and be roughly 20 percent larger and flatter than when you started.

Scooping Tilt the cleaver at an angle, with the sharp edge pointing away from you. Run the flat side of the blade underneath the prepared food in one movement and scoop up the pieces to place them on a serving platter or in a bowl or wok. Rest your hand lightly on top of the food to help it onto the cleaver if necessary.

Chopping To prepare boy choy, hold the stalk of the vegetable lightly with one hand. Place the cleaver at a slight angle, resting the side of the blade gently against the hand holding the bok choy. Measure the distance from the edge of meaty stalk for required size. Press down, and make clean cuts to separate leaf and stalk.

Shredding To make fine julienne slices of firm ingredients such as ginger, place the food on the cutting board and slice off the skin, removing the broadest sides first. Slice finely, keeping the food in one piece as much as possible. Place several slices on top of each other, and cut through the layers to make fine shreds.

Crushing Smash the cloves of garlic with the broad, flat side of the blade and the skin will slide off smoothly. Apply pressure with one hand on the blade's flat side near the blunt edge, and crush the garlic to the desired size. Rapid chopping will produce minced garlic, but less juice will be produced than when crushing.

easy vegetable stir-fries

mushrooms with bamboo shoots
Soak 6 dried Chinese mushrooms until soft. Squeeze out the water, discard the stalks, and cut into quarters. Halve 6 straw mushrooms. Cut ½ cup bamboo shoots into ½-inch strips. In a wok, heat 2 tbsp. oil and stir-fry 1 tbsp. crushed garlic for 1 minute. Add bamboo shoots and cook 2 minutes. Add mushrooms and stir-fry 1 minute. Add 2 tbsp. sesame oil, 1 tbsp. light soy sauce, 1 tsp. pepper, ⅓ cup water mixed with 1 tsp. cornstarch, and 2 tbsp. Chinese wine. Bring to a boil and serve immediately.

sichuan four harmonies
Slice a large carrot diagonally and blanch it in boiling water for 2 minutes. Cut a yellow bell pepper into pieces the same size as the carrot. Quarter a large red onion. Fry 1 tbsp. crushed garlic and 1 tsp. crushed ginger in 2 tbsp. oil for 1 minute. Add 1 tbsp. sesame oil and the onion and stir-fry 2 minutes. Add the carrot, pepper, 16 snow peas, plus 1 tbsp. light soy sauce, and stir-fry 2 minutes. Mix ⅓ cup water with 2 tsp. cornstarch and add to the wok with 2 tbsp. rice wine. Bring to a boil and serve.

bean sprouts with scallions
Wash 1⅔ cup bean sprouts and drain thoroughly. De-seed 2 large green chili peppers and cut into narrow strips. Slice 4 scallions into 2-inch lengths. Heat 2 tbsp. of oil in a wok and toss the scallions in it for 30 seconds. Add the bean sprouts and chili peppers, and stir-fry over high heat for 1 minute. Add 1 tsp. salt and continue stir-frying for a further 30 seconds, then serve hot.

celery with straw mushrooms
Trim off the root end of a whole head of celery and trim off the leaves. Cut the stalks into 2-inch lengths, then julienne. Wash and drain ⅔ cup canned straw mushrooms. Heat 2 tbsp. of oil in a wok and stir-fry the celery for 1 minute. Add the straw mushrooms and continue stir-frying over a high heat for 2 minutes. Add 1 tsp. salt and 2 tbsp. water and stir continuously until the water comes to a fast boil. Serve hot.

woks and their accessories

The wok has a mystical history dating back 3,000 years, yet in all that time it has never changed its ingenious shape. Riding on the popularity of stir-frying as a healthy cooking method, it is now endorsed by chefs of many nationalities and can be a best friend in the home kitchen as well, serving as a deep-fryer, steamer, braiser, and Dutch oven all in one.

1, 3 **Woks** Woks today come in a wide range of materials and sizes. The best are made of heavy cast iron and normally need only be seasoned before use. New ones, however, must be filled with oil and heated through before being drained and dried. For other metals prone to rusting, use a metal scouring pad to remove any traces of rust before you start cooking. Nonstick woks are not suited for rapid stir-frying, because the action of the ladle may chip the pan's synthetic coating. A wok made from stainless steel will conduct heat very rapidly, so it is liable to burn food too easily. Electric models are not ideal for stir-frying because they conduct heat at a rapid and uneven rate, though they are good for braising and steaming. Choosing a single- or double-handled wok is largely a matter of preference. One-handled versions are favored by restaurants because they allow the chef to easily toss large quantities of ingredients during stir-frying, which helps the action of the wok ladle.

2 Wok lid Wok lids are required for braising, steaming, and smoking. They are also used to facilitate the stir-frying process. When placed on the wok during cooking, they create a flash of dense moist heat, thereby speeding up cooking.

4 Wok·stand The wok's round base does not sit well on stove tops. These circular stands, typically made of iron, have four teeth strategically placed to grip the crossbars of the stove, allowing the wok to sit firmly.

The wok's shape ensures that heat is concentrated at the base and is less intense on the sides, perfect for stir-frying. A flat-based skillet simply does not do the job as well. Avoid "modern" re-interpretations of the timeless design. To get the most out of your wok, familiarize yourself with its accompanying tools, which help turn it from simple pan into multitasking wonder-cooker.

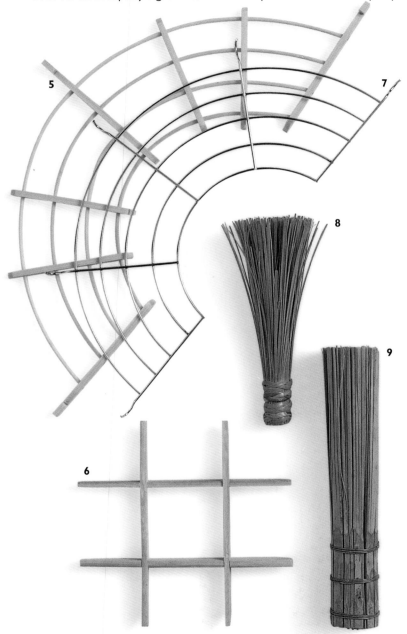

5, 7 Draining racks These come in bamboo or metal and are placed on the side of the wok to drain deep-fried food, such as spring rolls. Hooks at the end of each crossbar help to keep it steady.

6 Steaming trivet Originally made of bamboo or wood, steaming trivets are now often metal. These simple grids of two crossbars rest at the bottom of the wok and cradle plates and bowls during steaming, keeping them above the boiling water.

8, 9 Bamboo wok-cleaning brushes A precursor of the plastic scrubbing brush, this is no more than a bunch of bamboo or thin wooden battens bundled together to form a thick brush that is both comfortable to hold and easy to use. Excellent for removing stubborn stains and charred grit, these attractive cleaning brushes come in various sizes.

10 Long chopsticks These long, thick chopsticks, up to 18 inches in length, are used for manipulating

noodles and deep-fried foods in the wok. Their length allows the cook to keep a safe distance from splattering hot oil, while the string at the top helps to keep them manageable and maneuverable.

11 Wok ladle The wok ladle or "spatula," looks like a miniature shovel. There is total logic to this design, because the size and shape correspond exactly to the base of the wok, so that in one scooping motion, almost all the food can be tossed and turned for effective stir-frying. The slightly raised sides prevent spillage, and the angle of the head corresponds to the gradient of the wok. Wok ladles are traditionally made of rust-resistant metal or have wooden handles. They are now available in stainless steel or wood and are sometimes slotted to aid draining.

how to stir-fry

Making this classic vegetable dish of bok choy with ginger and oyster sauce provides a good opportunity to practice your stir-frying technique. For best results, prepare all the ingredients before starting to cook, get the oil really hot, and keep the food constantly moving in the wok.

Step 1. Trim the hard stalk ends of 7 oz. bok choy and cut the rest into 2-inch pieces. Peel a small piece of fresh ginger and slice 1 tbsp. of fine shreds. Heat 2 tbsp. oil in a wok until very hot. Add the ginger and stir with wok ladle until it is light brown.

Step 2. Add the firm, white stem sections of bok choy and continue cooking over high heat for 2 minutes. Use the ladle to constantly flip the ingredients away from the hot base of the wok, moving the food rapidly around the wok so that it doesn't overcook.

Step 3. Stir in the green leafy parts of the bok choy, then add 1 tbsp. oyster sauce and ⅓ cup water. Continue stir-frying until the liquid comes to a rapid boil. Transfer to a serving dish—the wok's sloping sides make this easy—and serve hot.

peking-style caramel walnuts

Although these delicious "lacquered" nuts are best started the day before serving, they are well worth the effort. They can be served hot or cold and make a great conversation piece at cocktail parties. Cashews can be used instead of, or as well as, walnuts if preferred.

Serves 8

Preparation time: 25 minutes, plus 2–12 hours drying

Tools	Ingredients
Pot	2 cups shelled
Colander	English walnuts
Baking tray	⅔ cup sugar
Wok	2 cups oil
Wire strainer	6 tbsp. sesame seeds
Wire rack	

Method

1. Bring a large pan of water to a boil, add the walnuts, and simmer uncovered for 5–10 minutes or until the water turns dark and the nuts start to turn pale. Drain and rinse the walnuts under a cold tap until the water runs clear.
2. Dry the nuts thoroughly with paper towels and spread them out on the baking tray. Pour the sugar evenly over them, then roll the nuts in it so that they are completely coated. Place the tray in a cool place, preferably in a light breeze, and leave to dry overnight, or for a minimum of 2 hours.
3. When ready to proceed, heat the oil in the wok to a moderate heat. Divide the nuts into small batches so that the pan is not crowded. Add the first batch to the oil and cook for 2 minutes or until the sugar melts and the nuts are golden.
4. Using a wire mesh strainer, lift the nuts from the oil and lay them on the wire rack, keeping them well separated. Sprinkle with some of the sesame seeds.
5. Repeat with the remaining walnuts and serve warm or cold. Alternatively, the caramelized nuts can be kept in a closed jar for up to 2 weeks.

wok cooking techniques

The wok's versatility obviates the need for a battery of utensils for different methods of cooking. However, it is helpful to have two woks, of 10 inches and 12 inches in diameter respectively. The larger one is better for holding bamboo steamers and for smoking; the smaller can be used for deep-frying and braising. They can be stored stacked one inside the other, taking up less room.

Deep-frying The wok's curvature means it requires much less oil for deep-frying than a conventional deep-fryer. Place a draining rack on the side of the wok. Add oil to one-third up the sides of the wok and heat well. Fry a few pieces of food at a time. When done, remove each item, holding it at an angle so that the excess oil drains away. Place on the draining rack to drain completely before transferring to a serving dish.

Tea-smoking Smoking involves low, gentle heating for cooking and flavoring foods that are not too thick or dense, such as fish or thin slices of meat and poultry. Fill the wok with uncooked rice to a depth of one third mixed with a few handfuls of barley. Sprinkle with 1 tbsp. black or green tea. Wrap the food well in a double layer of foil and lay it directly on the grains. Cover with the wok lid and leave over low heat for about 1 hour to smoke, opening the foil package for the last 30 minutes of cooking. Avoid using highly flavored teas, such as Lapsang souchong, for smoking.

Steaming You can steam foods in a wok simply by placing food on a dish resting on the steaming trivet. Choose a dish large enough to sit steadily on the trivet, but allow room on the sides for easy removal. Fill the wok with water to just below the base of the dish. Bring to a boil, cover with the wok lid, and allow the steam to circulate. Alternatively, use a bamboo steamer of a diameter only slightly smaller than that of the wok. Ensure that it sits at least 2 inches above the water level, and cover with the steamer's own lid.

Braising The technique of braising involves cooking food gently in a well-flavored liquid in a closed container. The liquid should barely cover the main ingredients. The long, gentle simmering process will reduce it by about one half. Open the lid occasionally during cooking to check the evaporation rate and top off with a little liquid if necessary. When the food is cooked, remove it and reduce the gravy further by boiling vigorously until thickened, which will also intensify the flavor.

fish in chili bean sauce

British-born writer and radio journalist **fuchsia dunlop** speaks fluent Mandarin and trained to be a chef in Chengdu. This dish from her highly acclaimed book *Sichuan Cookery* is one of her personal favorites and beautifully demonstrates the region's famous love of chili.

Serves 4
Preparation time: 30 minutes

Tools	Ingredients
Cleaver	I whole carp, trout, or gray mullet
Cutting board	(about I lb. 10 oz.)
Large dish	¾ cup peanut oil
Wok and ladle	*For the marinade*
Wok lid	¾ tsp. salt
Small bowl	I–2 tbsp. Shaoxing wine

For the sauce

4 tbsp. Sichuan chili bean paste
I tbsp. minced fresh ginger
I tbsp. minced garlic
1¼ cups chicken broth
I tsp. white sugar
I–2 tsp. light soy sauce
¾ tsp. potato starch
½ tsp. Chinkiang or black Chinese vinegar
3 scallions, green parts only, finely sliced

Method

1. Use the cleaver to make 4 or 5 shallow diagonal cuts on each side of the fish, and pierce the head. Place in a large dish and rub the fish inside and out with the salt and Shaoxing wine. Leave to marinate while you assemble the other ingredients.

2. In the wok, heat ⅓ cup of oil over high heat until smoking. Dry the fish with paper towels and sauté it briefly on each side for just long enough to crisp the skin. Remove and set aside. Rinse and dry the wok.

3. Return the wok to medium heat and add 4 tbsp. fresh oil. When hot, add the chili bean paste and stir-fry 20–30 seconds, or until the oil is red and smells delicious. Add the ginger and garlic and stir-fry for about 20 seconds or until you can smell their fragrance. Add the broth, increase the heat, and bring the liquid to a boil. Season to taste with the sugar and soy sauce.

4. Carefully place the fish in the wok and spoon some sauce over it. Reduce the heat, cover, and simmer 8–10 minutes, or until the fish is cooked and has absorbed some of the flavors of the sauce. Turn the fish once during cooking, spooning more sauce over it.

5. Carefully remove the cooked fish and place on a serving platter. In a small bowl, dissolve the potato starch in I tbsp. cold water and add to the sauce, stirring briefly until it thickens. Add the vinegar and scallions, stir a few times, then pour the sauce over the fish on the serving platter and serve.

braised five-spice belly pork

Originally from Northern China, this popular dish has transcended the provincial borders and is now prepared in almost every Chinese kitchen. In the north, it is traditionally served with a steamed bread known as *man dou*, whereas in the south it is most commonly served with rice.

Serves 4
Preparation time: 45 minutes

Tools	Ingredients	Method
Cleaver	2 tbsp. oil	**1.** Heat the oil in the wok and add the sugar. Cook until the sugar caramelizes and turns light brown, then add the pork slices. Turn them in the mixture until they are well coated.
Cutting board	1 tbsp. sugar	
Wok and ladle	2 lb. belly pork, sliced	
Wok lid	5 tbsp. dark soy sauce	**2.** Add the soy sauce, five-spice powder, water, and salt. Cover and cook gently over a low heat for 40 minutes, turning once or twice during braising. Add more water if necessary.
	2 tsp. five-spice powder	
	1 qt. water	**3.** Adjust the seasoning by adding extra soy sauce to taste, then serve.
	1 tsp. salt	

yang zhou fried rice

Fried rice must be the best-traveled Chinese dish of all time. It turns up in a myriad of guises around the world, even though it derives from the pragmatic need to recycle leftovers. This classic version is believed to have originated from the city of Yang Zhou and is positively ambrosial, with lots of premium ingredients, including roast pork, crabmeat, and shrimp.

Serves 4

Preparation time: 20 minutes

Tools	Ingredients	Method
Fork	2¾ cups cold cooked rice	**1.** Give the cold cooked rice a thorough raking to separate the grains. Devein the shrimp, making a deep slit down the back of each one.
Cleaver	⅔ cup raw shrimp, peeled	
Cutting board	2 tbsp. oil	
Wok and ladle	2 scallions, chopped, plus extra to garnish	**2.** Heat the oil in the wok and fry the scallions for 1 minute. Push them to one side of the pan.
	3 eggs, beaten	**3.** Add the beaten eggs to the pan, and cook until set. Remove from the wok and chop coarsely.
	⅔ cup roast pork or cooked ham, diced	**4.** Add the rice, shrimp, pork or ham, and crabmeat. Stir-fry vigorously for 3 minutes.
	⅔ cup crabmeat	
	2 tbsp. frozen green peas	**5.** Add the frozen peas, soy sauce, and pepper. Sprinkle the broth granules into the wok. Stir-fry 3 minutes more, then serve garnished with the extra chopped scallion.
	2 tbsp. light soy sauce	
	1 tsp. black pepper	
	1 tbsp. broth granules	

cooking pots

Although the wok reigns supreme in every Chinese kitchen, stir-frying is by no means the only cooking method. Various types of pots play important roles in the preparation of stocks, stews, and braised dishes. A good broth is very important to Chinese soups, but the wok's open shape and rapid evaporation rate make it unsuitable for broth making. One-pot dishes are favorite meals among many rural Chinese families, especially in colder regions.

1 Soup pot Soup and broth play important roles in Chinese cuisine, so large conventional cooking pots, much the same as those used in Western kitchens, are necessary. The most basic pot used would be a plain aluminum one; however, modern soup pots are made of stainless steel, and some have see-through lids.

3 Double-boiler This ancient Chinese utensil is much like a French bain-marie, and is used for slow simmering and stewing. This example is enameled. A lower pot holds water and also cradles a slightly smaller upper container in which the food is cooked. Each has a separate handle, and the top one has a tight-fitting lid. In ancient times in China, the double-boiler was used only for stews that required long, slow, and gentle cooking from an indirect heat source. Today, such pots are widely used in Southeast Asia to make sweet coconut custards.

2 Clay or sand pots The name of these lidded pots refers to their rough exterior. They come with either one or two handles and can be either glazed or unglazed. These pots need gentle handling, because they are delicate and will crack easily if placed on intense heat. They can be used directly on an electric ring or ceramic hotplate but not on a gas burner, unless a heat diffusion mat is used. The wire frame surrounding the pot is intended to help to protect it from breaking. Clay pots serve as an oven-to-table utensil when food must be presented piping hot or still sizzling. The best way to use them is to cook the dish in a conventional wok and then transfer it to a clay pot that has been preheated in a very hot oven for 30 minutes. The pots come in several sizes, ranging from large enough to contain a whole duck to small enough for one portion of stew or a braised dish. Anything cooked in such a pot must contain a proportion of liquid. Always use a wooden spoon with clay pots, because metal will scratch the fragile interior. To protect your face from the release of steam, lift the lid away from you when you remove it from the pot.

4 Hunan pot Originating from the province of Hunan, these finely crafted, delicate clay or terra-cotta pots with funnels in the center are typically used for ritual purposes. They were originally containers for medicinal brews and herbal soups that only well-to-do families could afford. Hunan pots are not robust enough to be placed on direct heat, and herbal soups are only poured into them after being cooked in other pots.

double-boiled black chicken soup with shark's fin and sea cucumber

Black chicken is a special genus of the bird that has jet-black skin but is like any other chicken in flavor. The Chinese believe it to have rejuvenating properties. This version of the popular medicinal dish is from chef peter tsang of the Shang Palace at the Shangri-la Hotel, Singapore.

Serves 6

Preparation time: 3 hours 15 minutes

Tools	Ingredients
Cleaver	1 black chicken
Cutting board	4 oz. sea cucumber
Large pot	1½ oz. ginseng
Colander	⅓ cup shark's fin, soaked
Double-boiler	1 tsp. salt
	½ tsp. pepper
	5 red dates
	4 slices ginger

Method

1. Clean the chicken and blanch it in a pot of boiling water for 3 minutes. Drain in a colander. Meanwhile, slice the sea cucumber into ¼-inch pieces and cut the ginseng into strips or slices.

2. Place the blanched chicken in the top part of a double-boiler with 4½ cups water. Add the sea cucumber and ginseng, plus the shark's fin, salt, pepper, red dates, and sliced ginger.

3. Fill the bottom part of the double-boiler with water up to the halfway mark. Cover the top part and simmer for 3 hours over low heat. Check periodically to make sure there is still water in the bottom part and top off if necessary.

4. Transfer to a serving dish and serve.

tung-po mutton

Su Tung-Po (A.D. 1036–1101) was a poet, painter, calligrapher, and epicure. A native of Sichuan, he spent most of his life traveling around China and is credited with the invention of this famous dish. This version comes from cooking author and teacher deh-ta hsiung, who has written dozens of authoritative books on Chinese cuisine.

Serves 4

Preparation time: 1 hour

Tools	Ingredients
Cleaver	4 tbsp. oil
Cutting board	14 oz. boneless mutton
Wok and ladle	or lamb, cubed
Deep pot	2 large potatoes, cubed
	1 large carrot, cubed
	2 tbsp. dark soy sauce
	1 tbsp. ginger paste
	1 tsp. five-spice powder
	⅓ cup Chinese wine or sherry
	1 tsp. sugar
	1 tsp. salt
	4 cups water

Method

1. Heat the oil in a wok and sauté the meat until the surfaces are sealed. Remove and set aside to drain on a paper towel.

2. Fry the potatoes in the remaining oil until light brown. Add the carrot and fry for 2 minutes. Remove the vegetables and set aside.

3. Transfer the meat, seasonings, and water to a deep pot and simmer, covered, for 40 minutes, or until the gravy has thickened.

4. Add the potatoes and carrot and continue cooking for 15 minutes more, then serve hot.

clay pot rice with salt fish and chicken

This traditional Cantonese dish successfully combines seafood with meat and is redolent with ginger, garlic, and sesame oil. Salt fish is much loved in China, not only as a savory ingredient but also as a fragrant salting agent, obviating the need for salt. Generally, a small amount is used, cut up into small pieces so the salt content is well distributed in the dish.

Serves 4
Preparation time: 45 minutes

Tools	Ingredients	Method
Clay pot	1 scant cup jasmine rice, washed	**1.** Preheat the oven to 475°F and place the clay pot in it to heat through while you cook.
Rice cooker	3 cups water	
Cleaver	1 chicken breast	**2.** Boil the rice in the water for 12 minutes. Meanwhile, cut the chicken into 1-inch cubes, slice the sausages diagonally into pieces ⅛ inch thick, and dice the salt fish.
Cutting board	2 Chinese sausages	
Wok and ladle	5½ oz. salt fish fillet	
	3 tbsp. oil	**3.** Heat the oil in a wok and sauté the ginger and garlic until light brown. Add the chicken, sausage, fish, sesame oil, oyster sauce, dark soy sauce, and pepper and toss well for 4 minutes.
	2 tbsp. grated ginger	
	3 cloves garlic, sliced	
	2 tbsp. sesame oil	
	2 tbsp. oyster sauce	**4.** Combine the contents of the wok with the cooked rice and transfer to the heated clay pot. Garnish with the chopped scallions and serve.
	2 tbsp. dark soy sauce	
	1 tsp. black pepper	
	2 tbsp. chopped scallions	

steamers and related tools

The method of steaming food is steeped in Yin Yang philosophy. In China, the belief is that fried foods must be counteracted by those that contain less or no oil and are therefore healthier. Steaming uses minimal amounts of flavoring, allowing the natural flavors of the basic ingredients to be tasted. It is an excellent way of cooking the seafood that is prolific in Chinese coastal waters and inland rivers. Lean meats and lean poultry joints become more succulent and flavorful when steamed, and no nutrients are lost, as they are with boiling. Last but certainly not least, steaming is an easy procedure; there is hardly anything that can go wrong, so there are many good reasons to incorporate more steamed dishes into your culinary repertoire.

1 Bamboo steamers These steamers are traditionally made of woven bamboo and come in various sizes, ranging between 6 and 14 inches in diameter. The larger the steamer, the larger the wok or saucepan that needs to be used with it. Generally, 10-inch-diameter steamers will suffice for domestic cooking needs. The great thing about steamers is that you can stack them one on top of the other and cook various foods using the same steam power. Steamers need only be rinsed in cold water and dried after use. Never use detergents to wash bamboo steamers because they absorb cleaning agents.

2 Lotus leaves The large, dried leaf of the lotus plant looks like a large gray-green fan, measuring about 16 inches in diameter. After soaking, it becomes tough and pliable, making it suitable as a wrapper for all kinds of foods, to which it imparts a faint floral perfume during steaming. The lotus plant is revered by Buddhists and Taoists and is symbolically related to the Goddess of Mercy, Kwan Yin, the protectress of seafarers.

3 Aluminum steamer
This modern version of the bamboo steamer also comes in multiple layers and has a high domed lid, but there is also a base section to hold water, so there is no need for a wok. Although useful for similar steaming operations, the lid is not perforated and tends to create too much condensation. This causes water to drop back onto the food and results in excess liquid in the dish. Prevent this by using the aluminum steamer in conjunction with the lid of a bamboo steamer, or puncture several small holes on the metal lid to create a vent.

4 One-portion aluminum steamer This is a handy small steamer for cooking dim sum and for reheating. It is just large enough to hold two small dumplings. Several of these little steamers can fit inside a large bamboo steamer to keep individual dim sum servings hot, without letting them overcook.

5 Little metal cups These small cups are used for steaming individual portions of savory rice flour cakes, a popular Chinese street food. The cakes are taken from the mold and placed onto plates or dried palm leaves, or eaten with a spoon straight from the cup.

6 Winter melon Looking somewhat like pale, small watermelons, winter melons are important as a "cooling" food within the Yin Yang philosophy, which classifies foods as either cooling or heating. Winter melons are often found in restaurants specializing in traditional Chinese medicinal dishes. A favorite way to prepare them is to slice off the top, then hollow out the melon in order to use the flesh as food and the shell as a container. Filled with broth, meat, and its own diced flesh, the whole melon is then steamed gently until soft, removing the need for a cooking pot. Diners scoop out the cooked flesh and drink the aromatic soup.

glutinous rice in lotus leaf

Chinese chefs are adept at cooking glutinous rice, usually wrapped around savory mixtures and often swathed in lotus leaves. This is known as *Lor Mai Fun* in Cantonese. The dried leaves are fragile before cooking and need to be soaked in water until soft so that they are pliable.

Serves 4

Preparation time: 1 hour 30 minutes

Tools	Ingredients
Bamboo steamer	1¾ cups glutinous rice, soaked 1 hour in cold water
Plate	*For the stuffing*
Cleaver	2 tbsp. oil
Cutting board	2 cloves garlic, crushed
Wok and ladle	1 cup diced chicken
Lotus leaf	1 Chinese sausage, thinly sliced
Flat square presser	4 Chinese mushrooms, soaked and chopped
	8 canned Chinese chestnuts
	2 tbsp. light soy sauce
	2 tbsp. oyster sauce
	2 tbsp. sesame oil
	2 tsp. salt
	1 tsp. black pepper
	1 tbsp. dark soy sauce
	2 tbsp. minced scallions
	chili sauce, to serve *(optional)*

Method

1. Steam the soaked rice for 20 minutes, then set aside.
2. Heat the oil in the wok and fry the garlic for
2 minutes. Add the chicken and Chinese sausage
and stir-fry for 5 minutes. Add all other ingredients
and continue cooking for another 5 minutes. Sprinkle
a little water on top. Remove from the heat.
3. Soak the lotus leaf in hot water for a few minutes,
then remove and wipe dry. Trim away the hard stalk.
4. Spread the rice out on the lotus leaf to a thickness

of about ½ inch and use the presser to firm it up.
5. Pile the fried ingredients in the center (top picture).
6. Lift up two opposite sides of the lotus leaf, line them
up together, and fold them over twice (bottom left).
7. Gather the remaining sides and fold them so that the
edges tuck in and under (bottom right).
8. Pat firmly and turn over, so that the seam is underneath. Place on a plate in a bamboo steamer.
9. Cover and steam for 10 minutes. Unwrap and serve
straight from the leaf with chili sauce to accompany.

steamed winter melon soup

Winter melons are about the size of a small, round watermelon and are often used as a cooking pot as well as a container that is brought to the table. The ingredients for this nourishing soup are all contained within the scooped out melon, and the melon flesh should be eaten with the soup.

Serves 6
Preparation time: 1 hour

Tools	Ingredients
Large pot	5 cups water
Cleaver	⅓ cup pearl barley
Cutting board	1 cup cubed chicken breast
Whole winter melon	1 cup diced cooked or Chinese ham
Spoon	⅔ cup canned lotus seeds, drained
Bamboo steamer with high-domed lid	2 tsp. salt
	1 tsp. sugar
	thinly sliced scallions, to garnish (optional)

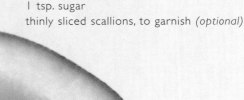

Method

1. Bring the water to a boil in the pot and simmer the barley for 15 minutes. Meanwhile, cut off the top third of the melon and reserve it to use as a lid. Discard the white connective tissue and seeds from the rind, and scoop out the melon meat, leaving about 1 inch of flesh in the shell.

2. Add the chicken, ham, and lotus seeds to the simmering barley and continue cooking for 15 minutes.

3. Transfer the contents of the pot to the melon shell and add the salt and sugar. Carefully sit the melon on a plate in the steamer. Replace the melon "lid" and cover the steamer tightly. Cook for 30 minutes. Bring the whole melon to the table with a few finely sliced scallions sprinkled over the soup if desired.

small cooking utensils

Although Chinese kitchens are not cluttered with equipment, there are a number of small tools that can be very handy for specific jobs. On occasions when you feel the urge to make special dishes and snacks like sweet tofu, homemade noodles, and steamed or fried vegetable cakes, these tools help to make the job a cinch.

1 Broth scoop Good broth or stock base (especially chicken) is essential to China's large variety of soups. This small aluminum bucket with a long handle is used to ladle the prepared broth from large, deep soup pots.

2, 4 Tofu scoops A plain round piece of metal, with or without a handle, serves as a scoop for tofu when portions need to be cut from a large slab. Commonly used in factories, they are also employed by Chinese street food vendors who scoop out individual portions of sweet tofu for their customers.

3 Flat square presser This aluminum square with a handle is used to press down steamed cakes made of mashed radish or yam to prevent air bubbles from forming during cooking.

5 Thread noodle slicer Noodles are fundamental to Chinese cuisines and are most commonly made from wheat or rice flour. Bean-thread vermicelli or cellophane noodles, made from mung bean starch, are also popular. Making fresh noodles at home in small quantities is relatively easy (it is very similar to making pastry or pasta), and the results taste so much better than store bought noodles. Chinese noodle makers make their noodles from rolled-out sheets of dough and cut them into varying widths with this tool. Wider ribbons are for soups, thinner for stir-fries. The slicer, a broad stainless steel blade measuring about 5 x 3 inches attached to a wooden handle, is used to cut and scoop up the strands of raw noodle dough.

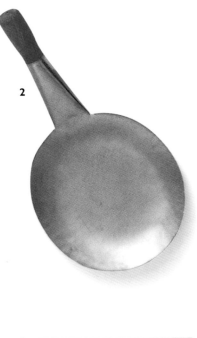

dim sum utensils

The term "dim sum" means "food to touch the heart." The range of dim sum foods is endless, especially when you consider that every regional Chinese cuisine has its own favorite recipes. There are, however, specific types of dishes, including fried, steamed, savory, and sweet, and also a small range of rice-based dishes, such as congee with century egg, salt fish, or chicken.

1 Cupcake molds Popular Chinese street food items, such as *chui kueh* (water cakes) or Little Buddhas (steamed rice cakes filled with a savory radish mixture), are made in these small aluminum cups.

2 Gelatin and tart molds These come in aluminum or plastic, with simple scalloped patterns, or in pineapple, fish, turtle, and rabbit shapes. Each motif is symbolic— pineapple for nobility (in Chinese the word sounds the same as the word for "emperor"), fish for rebirth, turtle for longevity, and rabbit for wisdom.

3 Reeded pastry brush Thin pieces of bamboo are fused together to make an easy-to-grasp handle for this broad, fine-haired brush, which is as functional as it is beautiful. It can be used for washing eggs and basting tarts and other festive cakes, as well as for lightly dusting with flour.

4 Wonton spreader A thin, short piece of finely whittled wood is used to scoop up and spread small amounts of ground pork or seafood when making wonton dumplings. The flat shape ensures that just enough of the filling mixture is placed on the wonton skins.

5 Dumpling dough roller This tool is much smaller and thinner than a conventional rolling pin and fits nicely into the palm of one hand, leaving the other free to manipulate the dumpling dough when rolling it out. The roller is made of light wood and is about 10 inches long.

mushroom and leek spring rolls

A long sojourn in France inspired esteemed American chef ming tsai of the Blue Ginger restaurant in Boston to devise this recipe, which uses leeks to give a French twist to traditional Chinese spring rolls. They make excellent party canapés.

Serves 4–6

Preparation time: 1 hour

Tools

Cleaver
Cutting board
Vegetable shredder
Medium bowl
Strainer or large sieve
Wok and ladle
Large spoon
Wire mesh ladle

Ingredients

3 oz. cellophane noodles
2 tbsp. oil, plus extra for deep-frying
1 tbsp. minced garlic
1 tbsp. minced root ginger
2 serrano chili peppers, minced
½ cup hoisin sauce
½ cup thinly sliced shiitake mushroom caps
2 large leeks, white parts only, very thinly sliced
8 tbsp. chopped fresh coriander
4 scallions, chopped
16 spring roll wrappers, about 8 inches square
1 egg, beaten with 4 tbsp. water
salt and black pepper

Method

1. Soak the cellophane noodles in a bowl of hot water for 10–15 minutes or until soft. Drain thoroughly, then chop them into pieces 2 inches long.
2. Heat the wok over high heat. Add the oil and swirl to coat the pan. When the oil is hot, add the garlic, ginger, and chili peppers, and cook until soft, about 2 minutes. Do not allow these ingredients to burn.
3. Reduce the heat to medium, add the hoisin sauce, and cook until it loses its raw taste, about 3 minutes. Add the shiitake mushrooms and leeks, and cook until soft, about 6 minutes. Season with salt and pepper.
4. Transfer the filling mixture to a strainer, and with a large spoon, press the mixture well to drain it thoroughly. Leave to cool.
5. Transfer the filling mixture to a medium-size bowl and add the coriander, scallions, and softened cellophane noodles. Stir to blend.
6. Dampen a kitchen towel. Place 5 wrappers on a work surface with one point of each near you, and cover the remainder with the cloth to prevent drying out.
7. Place about 4 tbsp. of the filling on the wrappers just above the nearest corner. Bring the corner nearest you up over the filling and roll halfway; fold in the side corners, brush the edges with egg wash, then continue rolling to enclose the filling completely, rolling as tightly as possible. Cover with the damp cloth and allow the rolls to rest seam side downward. Fill and roll the remaining wrappers, cover, and allow to rest at least 2 minutes.
8. Fill the cleaned wok one-third full with oil and heat to 350°F over high heat. Working in batches, fry the spring rolls until golden, turning as needed, for about 5 minutes. Remove with a wire mesh ladle and drain on paper towels. Slice the rolls diagonally or in half and serve hot with a dipping sauce.

potsticker techniques

These delightful dumplings, known as potstickers in China, are a relative of the Japanese gyoza. The dough is rolled out to be as thin as possible, but not so thin that the potstickers break when fried, because the crimped and pleated edges look nicer when the dough is fragile.

shanghai pork dumplings

The traditional method of cooking potstickers is to fry them until they are brown underneath and "sticking" to the pan, hence the name. A little water is then added to flash steam the dumplings until they are fully cooked, but add it carefully because it will splatter upon hitting the oil.

Serves 6

Preparation time: 45 minutes

Tools	Ingredients
Cleaver	3 scallions
Cutting board	12 oz. ground
Mixing bowl	pork
Small rolling pin	1 tsp. salt
Wonton	1 tsp. black
spreader	pepper
Skillet with lid	2 tbsp.
Wok ladle	sesame oil
	1 tbsp.
	cornstarch
	24 wonton
	wrappers
	oil for frying

Method

1. Finely chop the scallions and place in a mixing bowl with the ground pork. Add the salt, pepper, sesame oil, and cornstarch, and blend thoroughly so that the seasoning is well incorporated.

2. Using a wonton spreader, place a lump of mixture in the center of a wonton wrapper (top left). Dab around the edge of the wrapper with a little water (top center). Fold the wrapper over to make a half-moon shape, and seal sides firmly with the thumb and forefinger (top right).

3. Holding the sealed edge with both hands, make a pleat on one side of the dumpling (bottom left). Repeat to give 2 or 3 folds, much like the ruffle on a curtain (bottom center). Press down gently on the pleats so that they stay in shape (bottom right). Repeat with the remaining wonton wrappers and ground meat mixture.

4. Add a little oil to a skillet and heat it. Place about 6 of the dumplings in the pan, underside downward, pressing a little so that they sit firmly. Sauté the dumplings until the bases are brown.

5. Add about 2 tbsp. water to the pan, then quickly cover with a lid and steam-cook the dumplings until the pan is dry. Serve them hot with a dipping sauce of black vinegar and shredded ginger.

a moist, tender dough of exquisite thinness
encloses juicy seasoned ground pork and scallions
pan-fried to a golden richness

steamed shrimp shao mai

Shao mai is just one of hundreds of dim sum dishes. These delicate pea-topped dumplings are filled with savory ground shrimp flavored simply with ginger, garlic, scallions, and sesame oil. Wonton wrappers or "skins" are available ready-made from Chinese grocery stores.

Serves 4
Preparation time: 30 minutes

Tools	Ingredients
Cutting board	2 cups raw tiger shrimp, shelled
Cleaver	1 tbsp. garlic paste
Mixing bowl	1 tbsp. ginger paste
Steaming plate	2 tbsp. sesame oil
Wonton spreader	1 tsp. black pepper
Bamboo steamer	1 tbsp. cornstarch
Wok	1 egg, lightly beaten
	1 tsp. salt
	1 tbsp. light soy sauce
	2 scallions, finely chopped
	20–30 wonton wrappers
	30 large frozen garden peas

Method

1. On a cutting board, mince the shrimp with a cleaver until their texture resembles that of chopped nuts. Place in a mixing bowl with the garlic, ginger, sesame oil, pepper, and cornstarch, and stir well. Add the beaten egg, salt, soy sauce, and scallions, and mix thoroughly.

2. Using the wonton spreader, place a walnut-sized piece of filling onto a wonton wrapper (top). Then draw the sides up and shape into a little straight-sided dumpling (bottom). Trim off the ends of the wonton wrapper so that the edge is even with the filling. Place a single green pea in the center. Repeat with the remaining mixture and the rest of the wonton wrappers.

3. Place the shao mai on a lightly oiled steaming plate, making sure they do not touch. Fill the base of the steamer with water and bring to a boil. Place the plate in the steamer, cover, and cook for 20 minutes.

barbecued pork rolls

This item is a dim sum classic, a fluffy, light dough encasing savory-sweet roast pork or sometimes chicken. The same dough can be used to make sweet rolls: A spoonful of mashed red beans, sold canned in all Chinese stores, is placed in the center of the dough instead of meat.

Serves 4

Preparation time: 45 minutes, plus 2 hours rising time

Method

1. To make the dough, dissolve the sugar in the warm water and sprinkle with the yeast. Stir and leave for 15 minutes in a warm spot until a froth begins to form.

2. Sift the flour and salt into a large bowl. Add the yeast mixture and mix to a dough. Knead on a floured board for 15 minutes, or until the dough is elastic and smooth.

3. Place the dough in a warm, dry bowl and leave to rise in a warm spot for about 2 hours.

4. To make the filling, cut the pork into thick strips and marinate in the hoisin sauce, wine, and sugar for 10 minutes. Preheat the oven to 400°F.

5. Place the pork on a rack in a roasting pan and roast for 35 minutes. Cool and cut into ¼-inch cubes.

6. Shape the dough into a cylinder about 2 inches in diameter. Cut into rounds ¼ inch thick, then roll each into a thin circle 3 inches in diameter. Place 1 cube of roast pork in the center of a circle, then bring up the sides of the dough, and pinch to seal firmly. Repeat with the remaining circles.

7. Prepare a steamer by filling the base with water and bringing the water to a boil. Cut several squares of parchment paper the size of the base of the dumplings. Oil the paper lightly and place a dumpling on each square. Arrange the dumplings in the steamer, cover, and cook for 20 minutes. Serve hot or at room temperature.

Tools	Ingredients
Cleaver	*For the dough*
Cutting board	1 tsp. sugar
Mixing bowl	1 cup warm water
Fine sieve	2 tsp. active dry yeast
Small spoon	4 cups all-purpose flour
Steamer and lid	a pinch of salt
Wok	*For the barbecued pork filling*
Roasting pan with rack	8 oz. boneless lean pork
Pastry brush	2 tbsp. hoisin sauce
	2 tbsp. Chinese wine
	1 tsp. sugar

tableware

Unlike a formal meal in the West, where the flatware and hollowware depend on the kind of food on the menu, a Chinese table is set relatively simply, and the same implements are used regardless of the food served. Meals are generally communal, and a selection of different dishes is served together, with or without a central bowl of soup. The individual place settings consist of a rice bowl, chopsticks, and porcelain spoon, and the diners simply help themselves from the dishes available.

1 Teapot Tea is the favorite accompaniment to food in Chinese restaurants, although contrary to popular belief, it is rarely served with food in Chinese homes. The tea is placed in the pot and hot water added again and again as needed. The traditional shape of Chinese teapots is round and squat, though they are taking on other shapes as fashion changes.

2 Tea cups Tea is served in small cups and replenished often. When offered in the home as a refreshment for guests, the tea is presented with both hands and drunk the same way, hence the absence of saucers and handles.

3 Porcelain rice bowl The shape and size of traditional Chinese rice bowls have remained unchanged for centuries. To hold the bowl, place your thumb on the upper rim and four fingers on the lower rim. The bowl

is supposed to be held near the mouth, and rice delicately pushed in with chopsticks. Rice is not meant to be picked up a few grains at a time, because in China grains dropping between the chopsticks signify bad luck.

4 Soup noodle bowl Noodles are meant to be one-dish meals in and of themselves, and large bowls such as this are used for serving soup-based noodle dishes.

5 Small sauce dishes These come in various sizes and shapes, some compartmentalized so that they can contain a few items such as soy sauce, grated ginger, chili sauce, sliced chili peppers, mustard, or vinegar.

6 Dinner plate The Chinese do not serve rice on a plate except when entertaining Westerners who are not used to eating rice from a bowl. Plates such as this are used only when a one-dish meal is served, for example, fried noodles. However, such plates are commonly used in Southeast Asia and Indochina.

7 Soup bowl The traditional family method of eating soup is for all the diners to dip their spoons into a large, central bowl. Today, individual soup bowls such as this are a more common sight, thanks to modern hygiene requirements. Individual portions of congee are also served in this type of bowl.

8, 9 Porcelain spoon and rest Because porcelain conducts heat poorly, these are sensible implements for drinking hot soup. The soup is cooled as it is carried to the mouth, so the lips are not scalded. Such spoons are also used for mixing and stirring sauces and marinades containing vinegar, because a metal spoon will react with acidic ingredients. The spoon rest avoids staining the tablecloth.

10 Chopstick rest The porcelain chopstick rest helps to keep the food-stained tips of the chopsticks off the tablecloth. Elaborately decorated versions are one of the formal touches at banquets.

11 Chopsticks The regular chopsticks for eating are about 10 inches long, and are traditionally made from bamboo or wood. In ancient China, the imperial classes used ivory or even solid gold. Plastic chopsticks are not ideal for eating noodles, which are slippery. Lacquer chopsticks are intended for ornamental use rather than for eating, but they can be used for cold dishes.

12 Soup tureen A soup tureen is generally used for serving soup at the center of the table. It also makes an ideal container for serving stews. The lid keeps heat in effectively. There are no handles, so it is important to wear hot mitts when moving a hot tureen.

13 Soup ladle When soup is served as a main dish, a large porcelain ladle is used. It normally features a slightly curved handle and flat-bottomed bowl section.

14 Soy sauce bottle The Chinese equivalent of Western salt and pepper shakers, the soy sauce bottle is typical of restaurant rather than home use. It is placed on the dining table for individual seasoning of meals. However, in a Chinese home, any extra sauce is meant as a dip and presented in small dishes for shared use.

how to use chopsticks

Whether made of wood, bamboo, or elegant silver, chopsticks can be exasperating for those not familiar with using them. However, they can be mastered with a little practice at holding and clicking them together, and it will soon be easy to pick up even the tiniest, most slippery morsels.

Beginners will find bamboo or wooden chopsticks easier to use than plastic ones, and square-cut Chinese chopsticks easier to handle than pointed Japanese models. Practice clicking the chopsticks together before moving on to pick up food with them. The most important thing to remember is that only the top chopstick should move.

Step 1. Grasp one chopstick about a third of the way up, between the base of the thumb and the tip of the third finger. This chopstick must be kept steady throughout use. Some people (especially children) find it easier to hold them about halfway, but hold them too far back or forward and they will not provide enough leverage and will be unwieldy to use.

Step 2. Hold the second chopstick between the tips of the thumb, first, and second fingers, holding it above the other chopstick, again about a third of the way up. When the chopsticks are held parallel to each other, there should be a space of about ¾ inch between them.

Step 3. Keeping your thumb as the anchor, use the tip of your second finger to raise the front of the top chopstick, thus opening the set.

Step 4. Maintain control by holding the bottom chopstick steady, and use your second finger to lower the top chopstick, bringing the tips together with a light pressure so that you can grasp a piece of food.

hot-and-sour shrimp lo mein

Method

1. Peel, devein, and rinse the shrimp and set aside. Bring a small pan of water to a boil and blanch the water chestnuts for 10 seconds, then refresh under cold water, drain, and pat dry.
2. Bring a large pot of water to a boil, add the noodles, and cook until they are barely tender. Rinse under cold water in a colander, and set aside to drain thoroughly.
3. To make the ginger marinade, combine the Chinese rice wine, ginger, and sesame oil in a bowl. Add the shrimp, toss lightly to coat, and set aside. Make the hot-and-sour sauce in a separate bowl. Combine the broth, soy sauce, Chinese rice wine, sugar, vinegar, sesame oil, and cornstarch, then set aside.
4. Heat a wok over a high heat. Add 2 tbsp. of the oil and heat until very hot but not smoking. Remove the shrimp from the marinade and add them to the wok. Toss lightly for about 1½ minutes until they turn pink. Remove with a handled strainer and drain in a colander. Wipe out the wok.
5. Reheat the wok over a medium-high heat. Add the remaining 1½ tbsp. of oil and heat for about 20 seconds or until hot. Add the onion, garlic, and chili paste and stir-fry 1½–2 minutes or until the onion is slightly softened.
6. Add the water chestnuts and snowpeas, turn up the heat to high, and toss until heated through. Add the hot-and-sour sauce and cook, stirring constantly to prevent lumps, until the sauce has thickened, 2–3 minutes.
7. Add the shrimp and noodles and toss lightly. Transfer to a platter and serve immediately.

hot-and-sour shrimp lo mein

"When I was growing up, 'ordering Chinese' invariably meant lo mein noodles," says U.S. culinary expert nina simonds. "The Cantonese lo mein I loved as a child, however, bears little resemblance to this bright, fresh-tasting, and virtually greaseless version. Whenever I'm feeling nostalgic, I toss noodles in this spicy sauce laced with garlic, vinegar, and hot chilies."

Serves 6
Preparation time: 30 minutes

Tools	Ingredients
Cleaver	3 cups medium-size raw shrimp
Cutting board	¾ cup canned water chestnuts, drained and sliced
Small pot	8 oz. wide, flat noodles
Large pot	3½ tbsp. oil
Colander	1 medium red onion, thinly sliced
Small bowls	2½ tbsp. minced garlic
Wok and ladle	1 tsp. hot chili paste
Wire mesh strainer	1 cup snow peas, ends snapped, strings removed
	For the ginger marinade
	3 tbsp. Chinese rice wine or sake
	1½ tbsp. finely chopped fresh ginger
	1 tsp. sesame oil
	For the hot-and-sour sauce
	1⅓ cups Chinese chicken broth or water
	5½ tbsp. soy sauce
	2 tbsp. Chinese rice wine or sake
	2 tbsp. sugar
	2 tbsp. Chinese black vinegar
	1 tsp. toasted sesame oil
	1 tbsp. cornstarch

soup and congee

Most Chinese have a penchant for soups, derived from the Yin-Yang philosophy that they are sustaining because the ratio of substance to liquid is supposed to correct any bodily imbalance. Soups vary widely. Some are practically stews, containing plenty of meat, seafood, or noodles and are meant to be consumed as one-pot meals. Lighter soups have a different role to play as refreshing dishes or to help dry dishes go down well. Congee is a rice gruel, the staple of most rural communities in South China, and typical breakfast fare. It is traditionally made from broken rice grains. For variety, the basic mixture can be flavored with a wide range of tasty extras, such as lean fish, shredded chicken, mushrooms, dough sticks, cilantro, and sliced chili peppers.

chicken and mushroom soup

Cut 1 chicken breast into ¼-inch cubes. Wash 1 cup mushrooms under a cold faucet and cut into bite-sized pieces. Place the mushrooms and chicken in a pot with 3¼ cups water, 1 chicken bouillon cube, and 1 tbsp. light soy sauce. Bring to a boil and simmer 25 minutes. Add 1 tbsp. minced parsley and ½ tsp. black pepper, then serve hot.

congee with shrimp and scallions

Wash 1 cup jasmine rice thoroughly and place in a pot with 6 cups water. Bring to a boil, cover, and simmer for 40 minutes, or until the rice grains are very soft and the surrounding liquid is opaque white. Shell and clean ⅔ cup raw bay shrimp. Add them to the congee and simmer for 5 minutes. During the last minute, add 1 tbsp. sesame oil and ½ tsp. pepper. Garnish the congee with 2 tbsp. minced scallions just before serving.

japan
and
korea

japan and korea

Japanese culture may be difficult for non-Japanese people to fathom because of its near-mystical symbolism. However, the genius of Japanese cooking is its simplicity, the marrying of a few flavorings with the natural goodness of fresh ingredients, each dish a manifestation of the Japanese love of nature.

The objective of Japanese cooking is to let each ingredient, and each dish, reveal its own particular beauty and flavor. This may be by using a fall leaf as a garnish, artfully arranging a pickled vegetable, or carefully mixing and matching the colors of the china and lacquer serving dishes. It is this very simplicity that makes Japanese cuisine so enchanting. It imparts an almost Zen-like peace, with the focus not on quantity but on the revered essence of each morsel. The Japanese eat not only with their mouths but with their souls. Japanese diners contemplate every mouthful as though it were poetry.

The key flavorings used in Japanese cuisine are essentially simple. They include *dashi* (a broth flavored with fish flakes and seaweed), dried bonito, *sake*, plus soybean products such as soy sauces, and hundreds of different types of *miso*, a soy paste fermented with yeast. Other important Japanese ingredients are bamboo shoots, *daikon* (a large white radish), ginger, *shiitake* mushrooms, sheets of *nori* seaweed, *shirataki* noodles, and *soba* (buckwheat) noodles. Perhaps the most memorable taste for first-timers is *wasabi* paste, an extremely pungent condiment of green horseradish that makes you want to sneeze.

There are seven main types of cooking methods used in Japan. A typical meal will consist of a selection of small dishes, often three dishes, each made using a different cooking technique, plus miso soup, rice, and pickles. Broiled dishes are known as *yakimono*. Those most familiar to Westerners are *yakitori* and *teriyaki*. *Agemono* are deep-fried foods such as tempura. *Nimono* are simmered or poached foods—essentially the stews of Japanese cooking. *Mushimono* are steamed items, *itamemono* are sautéed or pan-fried, *sunomono* are vinegared, and *aemono* are dressed dishes often featuring a thick sauce.

The Japanese delight in serving foods in tandem with the seasons. The best Japanese restaurants maintain separate sets of dishes and serving utensils for each season. The pattern of the kimono and obi sashes worn by the waitress reflects the season—red for fall, white for winter, green for spring, and orange for summer. The ambience harmonizes with the dishes served, and food is arranged to reflect the shapes, colors, and textures of the seasons.

It is sushi that perhaps most captures Western imagination. Frequently confused with sashimi, which is simply raw fish, sushi is cooked sticky rice that has

ABOVE: **1** sushi rice, **2** kombu seaweed, **3** bonito powder, **4** hijiki seaweed, **5** seven-spices chili, **6** red chili pepper, **7** wakame seaweed, **8** nori seaweed, **9** udon noodles, **10** sesame seeds, **11** soba noodles, **12** black sesame seeds.
OPPOSITE: **1** daikon radish, **2** shimeji mushrooms, **3** shiso leaves, **4** spinach, **5** enoki mushrooms, **6** shiitake mushrooms, **7** edamame, **8** burdock root.

been flavored with vinegar and is often topped with pieces of raw fish or shellfish. It is either eaten as an appetizer or as an entrée. The Japanese consider raw fish to be the high point of a meal and all the dishes that follow are merely accompaniment. Sushi is an art form in itself, but does not have to be purist. Nor does it have to feature raw fish.

Up until the end of the sixteenth century, the island nation of Japan was almost completely isolated from the rest of the world. The first Europeans to reach its shores were Portuguese seafarers, who initiated a brisk trade between the two countries. Jesuit missionaries then began arriving, hoping to convert the Japanese to Christianity. They noticed, even then, that the Japanese consumed practically no meat and ate large quantities of rice and seafood. The Portuguese began to interfere with the Japanese feudal system. This, coupled with fear of an invasion by Spaniards based in the Philippines, caused them to be expelled in 1638. Foreigners were banned from the country, and Japanese were forbidden to leave on pain of death. Japan's doors were locked against the world until the arrival of Commodore Perry in the nineteenth century.

The Portuguese legacy in Japan is the recipes for deep-fried foods that came to be known as *tempura*. The word itself was the result of the Portuguese Catholics' rejection of meat on Ember Days, which they called by the Latin name of Quatuor Tempora, the "four times" of the year. They asked instead for seafood, usually shrimp. Eventually, the word *tempura* became attached to the fried

BELOW: **1** kimchee yangnyum, **2** umeboshi plums, **3** gochujang chili paste, **4** miso, **5** fried bean curd, **6** soy sauce, **7** mirin, **8** fresh tofu, **9** pickled daikon, **10** brown vinegar.

shrimp and it remains so to this day, although other foods such as salmon, tofu, bamboo shoots, and vegetables are also cooked tempura-style.

Korea is a peninsula with a cool, subtemperate climate that yields abundant produce. For centuries, Koreans have enjoyed the harvests of the sea, land, and mountains. Korean cuisine is fragrantly spicy and hearty. It is strongly flavored with garlic, ginger, black pepper, scallions, soy sauce, and sesame seeds. Chili peppers are used liberally, and bean paste, mustard, vinegar, and rice wine are also important ingredients. The permutations of these flavorings in marinades and seasonings are endless.

The staple dish for every Korean is *kimchee*, a spicy pickled cabbage, of which there are many versions. Often two or three varieties of kimchee are served as part of a meal. The pickling liquid is a blend of salt, chili powder, fresh red chili peppers, ginger, soy sauce, and sugar. Layer upon layer of sliced cabbage is placed in a stone jar, covered with several pieces of cheesecloth to allow the pickle to "breathe," and, after about a week, the jar is opened to emit an intoxicating fragrance.

Beef is the favorite meat in Korea, most frequently in the guise of *bulgogi* (chili beefsteak) or *bulgabi* (barbecued short ribs), served in *Yangyum kanjang*, a pungent mixture of soy sauce, sesame oil, bean paste, wine, scallions, chili paste, garlic, and sugar. The meats are marinated in this paste for several hours and then grilled over hot coals or cooked on a cast-iron griddle at the table.

The Koreans often use a fermented soybean paste similar to the Sichuan chili bean paste, known as *gochujang*. It has a surprisingly mellow flavor, given the amount of ground chili in it. Seaweed is used in many different ways, the Korean *kim* being similar to Japanese *nori*. They are used in much the same way—as a wrapper or shredded and added to soups.

Korea has some unique noodles in the form of *naengmyon*, a rubbery buckwheat noodle that is so long that the dried strands are folded in half and, when cooked, are cut with scissors at the table. The name means "cold noodle," and, although they can be served hot, they are most frequently featured floating in a cold soup.

In the past, poor farming families lived on a diet of boiled rice and vegetables, often eking out their supply of rice with the addition of other grains and legumes. The vegetables would be stir-fried in winter with a sharp seasoning such as chili and bean paste, and served cold and raw in summer. The Korean diet has changed much over the past few decades, and with more Koreans traveling abroad, as well as foreigners visiting the country, taste buds are being shaped by the introduction of international foods.

knives and cutting boards

Top-quality Japanese kitchen knives are truly the razor-sharp progeny of the Samurai fighting sword and are among the most prized possessions in Japanese homes. Forgers of these blades are regarded as living national treasures. Japanese knives are forged so that only one side of the blade has a cutting edge, usually on the right, so that they cut much faster and more cleanly than the double-edged knives typically used in the West. Two materials are favored—carbon steel and stainless steel. Carbon steel is superior and honed so sharply that it can actually split a hair. Always hold a Japanese knife lightly, not with a stranglehold. With the correct movement and rhythm, a knife is an extension of your hand, and there should be no awkward tension while cutting.

1. Kitchen carver Known as a *deba*, this functions like a Chinese cleaver but is narrower and lighter, usually measuring 7 inches long by 1¾ inches wide. It is basically used for trimming and filleting fish but can also be used for poultry and meats. Indeed, there is no reason why this versatile implement cannot be used for other jobs, including heavy chopping work.

2. Fish slicer Traditionally used for sashimi, this long, slender knife with a blunt end is known as a *tacobiki*, or octopus knife. It is ideal for slicing fish fillets, as well as cutting neat sushi rolls. Another type of sashimi knife, the *yanagi-ba* or willow-leaf blade, is also long and slender, but looks more like a Western knife because the blade ends in a fine point. Serrated knives will never do for slicing fish because they tear instead of making clean cuts. Always have a folded wet cloth close by and wipe the blade frequently to keep it clean while working.

3. Vegetable knife Shaped and weighted like a Chinese cleaver, albeit narrower, this is used mainly for vegetable cutting. Its weight and leverage make it suitable for delicate cutting, chopping, and fine slicing, and even crushing garlic. Choose brands made of carbon steel.

4. All-purpose knife With its 10-inch single-sided blade, this knife is a Japanese version of an all-purpose chef's knife and known as an *oroshi*. It can be used for preparing fish, beef, poultry, and vegetables. Like the others shown here, it has a nonslip, wooden handle and should be sharpened on a whetstone.

5. Cutting board The Japanese use conventional cutting boards, but chefs have a preference for square or rectangular shapes made of pine. Since the cuisine relies heavily on cutting, these tend to be larger than are normally seen in the West.

simple japanese pickled vegetables

Traditionally, Japanese pickled vegetables are much more than condiments. The art of pickling, known as *tsukemono*, is actually very extensive, each accompaniment being regarded with the same reverence as the entrée. Every Japanese home has its own pickling crock or barrel. Pickles are relished for their piquant, salty flavors that blend artfully with the taste of raw fish and unseasoned meats. They also have a cleansing effect on the palate and aid digestion.

pickled radish
Finely grate 1 large daikon. Sprinkle 2 tsp. salt all over the radish shreds and stir well. Let stand for 20 minutes, then squeeze out as much moisture from the daikon as possible. Add 2 tbsp. rice wine, 1 tbsp. sugar, and 1 tsp. sesame seeds and toss well.

pickled eggplant
Wash and dry 4 baby eggplant and quarter them lengthwise. Rub with 1 tbsp. salt and reserve on a piece of absorbent paper towel for at least 1 hour. Combine ⅔ cup miso, 2 tbsp. mirin, and 1 tbsp. finely grated ginger in a small bowl. Gently squeeze the moisture from the eggplant and place in a shallow bowl. Pour the pickling liquid over it, cover, and steep overnight or for several days. Serve with broiled fish or chicken.

pickled turnip
Peel 1 lb. large turnips, then rinse and cut into thin julienne strips. Place in a bowl and sprinkle liberally with 2 tbsp. salt. Set aside for 10 minutes, then squeeze the moisture from the turnip. Add 1 tbsp. kombu strips and 1 tbsp. grated lemon zest, and let stand for 30 minutes at room temperature. To serve, drain off any excess liquid and arrange in a mound next to fish or meat dishes.

sashimi

It is imperative that fish for sashimi be impeccably fresh. Place your fillet on a cutting board and hold the sashimi knife so that the blade is inclined slightly to the left. With a sweeping motion, draw the knife toward you from blade base to tip, applying gentle pressure but letting the weight of the knife do the work. Move the tip of the knife, with the piece of fish on it, slightly to one side and lay the fish on its side. Serve with shredded daikon, shiso leaves, and wasabi.

sushi equipment

While many people associate sushi with raw fish, the term actually means "vinegared rice" and consequently the rice preparation is the most important element. Having the proper tools makes all the difference for the results. The rice has to be cooled to the right temperature, and it must have the correct texture and sheen. Natural materials, such as bamboo and wood, have a special quality that ensures that the rice comes out perfect because, unlike metal, they do not react chemically with foods. Furthermore, it is virtually impossible to get the precise shape required for rolled sushi without using a genuine sushi mat.

1 Rice cooling tub Known as a *hangiri*, this is made from the wood of a special cypress tree and bound with copper hoops. Perfect for rapid cooling of sushi rice (which must always be freshly made), the wood also helps give the rice its proper gloss and malleable texture. The cooling process is aided by fanning the rice to drive out moisture and produce the right flavor.

2 Wooden spatula Far from being an arcane kitchen tool, this flat, round-ended spatula is regarded as an important symbol of the Japanese housewife's domain. Usually made of wood, but sometimes of decorative porcelain, it is used to turn and spread sushi rice. The wood imparts a faint flavor to the rice.

3 Fan Usually made of bamboo ribs covered with either paper or silk, this fan is used to cool rice for sushi and to coax a charcoal fire to produce embers.

4 Bamboo mat This 10-inch-square mat of thin bamboo is for forming and pressing rice and other soft foods into cylindrical shapes. A nori sheet is toasted and placed directly on the mat, and warm rice and flavorings are heaped on it and flattened. The mat is then rolled up, encasing the mixture. To avoid musty smells, wash the mat in tepid water after use, then wipe it. Allow it to dry completely before storing.

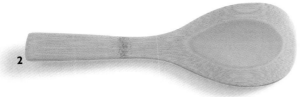

sushi

Japanese sushi chefs train for many years to perfect their craft, yet some types of sushi are easy to make at home. The rice may be shaped into oblongs and topped with a variety of seafood (known as *nigiri sushi*), or wrapped with sheets of nori seaweed.

Serves 4

Preparation time: 40–60 minutes

nori rolls

Tools	Ingredients
Sharp knife	de-seeded cucumber,
Cutting board	pickled daikon,
Bamboo mat	or fresh tuna fillet
Wooden spatula	2 sheets nori seaweed
	vinegared sushi rice
	(see recipe at right)
	½–1 tsp. wasabi paste
	pickled ginger and soy
	sauce, to serve

Method

1. Cut the de-seeded cucumber, pickled daikon, or fresh tuna into ¼-inch sticks, and set them aside.
2. Take a sheet of dry nori seaweed and gently warm it over a gas flame, holding it about 3 inches from the flame.
3. Place the bamboo mat on a dry cutting board and lay the toasted nori on top. Add 2–3 tbsp. of the cooked vinegared rice and gently spread it out over the nori until the thin layer of rice measures about 5 x 3 inches. Leave a gap of ½ inch between the edge of the rice and that of the nori.
4. Use your finger to smear a faint line of wasabi down the center of the rice, then cover it with a strip of your chosen filling.
5. Pick up the mat at the side nearest you and roll it over to meet the other side, enclosing the rice and filling inside the nori (see facing page). Roll the cylinder in the mat a little to help firm it up.
6. Remove the cylinder from the bamboo mat and set aside to rest, seam-side down, while you repeat the rolling process with the remaining ingredients.
7. Using a sharp knife, slice each cylinder into 1-inch pieces. Arrange the pieces of sushi on a serving platter and serve with pickled ginger, soy sauce, and a dab of extra wasabi paste if desired.

sushi rice

Tools	Ingredients
Colander	1¼ cups Japanese sushi rice
Electric rice cooker	¼ cup rice vinegar
Wooden cooling tub	1 tbsp. sugar
Fan	1 tsp. salt
Small saucepan	
Wooden spatula	

Method

1. Wash the rice and leave to drain for 30 minutes. Place it in the rice cooker with enough cold water to rise 1 inch above the level of the rice, then switch on the cooker. When done, transfer the cooked rice to the cooling tub.
2. Mix the vinegar, sugar, and salt in a small pan and place over medium heat until the sugar has dissolved. Cool using the fan.
3. Add the vinegar to the rice and mix gently for 2 minutes.

sushi techniques

Sticky rice is, as the name says, sticky. This can make it seem difficult to work it with your hands, because the grains stick to your fingers. The Japanese solution is to keep a bowl of acidulated water nearby, and to dip the hands in it before picking up the rice. To make this "hand vinegar," use 2 tbsp. rice vinegar for every ½ cup water.

rolling norimaki

Toasting nori seaweed over a gas flame darkens it and makes it more pliable for rolling.

Method

1. Place the bamboo mat on a dry chopping board and lay the toasted nori on top. Add 2–3 tbsp. of the cooked, vinegared rice and gently spread it out over the nori until the layer of rice is thin. Leave a ½-inch gap around the edge of the rice. Fill as desired.
2. Pick up the bamboo mat on the near side and roll it over to meet the other side, enclosing the rice in the nori and ensuring that the filling is in the center of the roll.
3. Lift the bamboo mat a little, then press it gently down and over the cylinder. Roll the cylinder in the mat a little to help the sushi firm up. Pat both ends in firmly and trim away the excess seaweed.
4. Lay the nori roll on the cutting board, seam side down. Using a sharp knife, cut into 1-inch pieces.

rolling uramaki

Also known as inside-out sushi, uramaki are a pretty alternative to norimaki and have the crunch and nutty taste of sesame. The secret of success is to use plastic wrap with your bamboo mat.

Method

1. Cover the bamboo mat with plastic wrap and set aside.
2. Toast the sheet of nori as directed for norimaki (see recipe left), then place it on a cutting board and spread with vinegared sushi rice, patting it out right to the edges of the seaweed.
3. Scatter 1 tbsp. of white or black sesame seeds (or a mixture of the two) evenly over the layer of rice.
4. Pick up the layered nori and turn it over onto the bamboo mat, so that the seeded side lies on the plastic wrap.
5. Arrange your chosen fillings, such as pieces of pitted *umeboshi* plum or finely shredded carrot and cucumber, in a line along the center of the seaweed.
6. Roll up into a cylinder using the method shown earlier for norimaki, then cut each cylinder of sushi into 1-inch pieces and serve.

hand-shaping nigiri sushi

This type of hand-molded sushi looks relatively easy to make, however the Japanese consider it one of the most difficult types to get exactly right, and usually leave it to the skills of the professional sushi chef. It takes trained hands to shape the rice gently but firmly so that it is cohesive enough to pick up in one piece while still being deliciously light-textured once inside the mouth.

Method

1. Wet your hands with acidulated water to prevent the rice from sticking. Take a handful of cooked, vinegared rice and mold it into a neat cylinder measuring about 2 x ¾ x ¾ inches. Using your finger, smear a little wasabi paste along the top of the rice.
2. Cover with a piece of thinly sliced raw tuna, salmon, sea bream, or skinned squid, cut so that it measures about 3 x 1 inches. Alternatively, top the molded rice with a cooked tiger shrimp, peeled and butterflied so that it sits flat on the rice. You can also make nigiri sushi with rolled omelet (page 58), cutting it into pieces measuring 3 x 1 x ¼ inches, and wrapping it with a thin strip of nori. In this case, omit the wasabi paste.

the cool softness of sticky rice, the crunch of nori seaweed
and sesame seeds, the tang of pickled ginger, and
the heat of wasabi: sushi is a perfectly balanced snack.

rice cookers, pots, and pans

The Japanese are extremely fond of simmered dishes that are not unlike the casseroles of Europe. Indeed, a full and well-balanced Japanese meal will always contain a simmered dish, along with something broiled, something steamed, a few deep-fried morsels, a sautéed dish, and a platter of vinegar-marinated foods or dressed salad. These pots and pans help to produce a real feast.

1 Omelet pan Known as a *makiyaki-nabe*, the Japanese omelet pan is oblong or square with a wooden handle, and is essential for the preparation of rolled egg dishes (*dashimaki*) for which the Japanese are renowned. Omelet pans can be made of heavy copper with a tin coating (the most expensive kind), cast iron, or heavyweight aluminum with a nonstick surface. They should be used for nothing but eggs and seasoned with a little oil before each use.

2 Earthenware pot Slow-cooked dishes are traditional to Japanese cuisine, for which the favored utensil is an earthenware pot or Dutch oven called a *do nabe*. It is often intricately patterned because it is taken directly from the oven to the table.

3 Japanese rice cooker Although this utensil is used throughout Asia, it is a Japanese invention, first produced about 80 years ago. Over the decades, the

basic pot has been modernized and altered to serve the purpose better, with all sorts of innovations including thermostatic control and its own heating element. The rice cooker consists of an inner aluminum pot inside an outer pot that has a spring-loaded base. Heat is generated around the sides between the two pots. The rice cooker works on the principle of weight; when all the water has been absorbed, the inner pot, now lighter, springs up, automatically shutting off the electrical power. No more burned or scorched rice! Electric rice cookers can be used for making soups, but in this case they have to be switched off manually. They can even be used for Korean firepot and fondue dishes. Sizes range from small models for two people to huge catering cookers for feeding for up to 50 people.

4 Tempura pan Some people think the Chinese wok can be used for making tempura, but this is not true. A Japanese tempura pan has straighter sides and is designed to keep the oil at an even temperature, imperative for perfect tempura. A wok, on the other hand, maintains different temperatures at different points and is too erratic for delicate deep-frying. Tempura pans come with their own racks so that the fried food can be placed on the side to drain.

5 Drop lid Known as an *otoshibuta* in Japan, this wooden lid, normally made of cedar, is placed inside saucepans during cooking. This helps to concentrate the heat in the food being cooked and stop the food from moving around and breaking up during boiling.

tempura shrimp

Japanese chefs have made deep-frying into an art form. Only the best oil is used, and the result-ing foods are remarkably grease-free, crisp on the outside, and perfectly cooked on the inside. The secret lies in the feather-light batter made at the very last moment before frying. This recipe can be easily adapted to cook almost any vegetable tempura-style.

Serves 4

Preparation time: 40 minutes

Tools	Ingredients
Knife	8 tiger shrimp, shelled, tails left on
Cutting board	oil for deep-frying
Tempura pot	grated daikon, soy sauce, and
Large bowl	wasabi paste, to serve
Fine sieve	*For the batter*
Small bowl	3 tbsp. all-purpose flour,
Bamboo draining basket	plus extra for dusting
Cooking chopsticks	1 tbsp. cornstarch
Grater	½ tsp. baking powder
	2½ cups ice-cold water
	1 large egg white

Method

1. Devein the shrimp and make a deep slit down the back. Spread out each shrimp like a butterfly and press down gently.
2. Heat the oil to 360°F. To test the temperature, fry a cube of bread; if it turns golden brown in 1 minute, the oil is ready.
3. Meanwhile, make the batter. Sift the flour, cornstarch, and baking powder into a bowl. Add the ice-cold water a little at a time, whisk-ing to combine.
4. In a separate bowl, beat the egg white until stiff peaks form, then fold it into the batter.
5. To cook, dip each shrimp into a little flour and then into the batter and deep-fry for 2–3 minutes.
6. Drain on a paper towel and serve with grated daikon, soy sauce, and wasabi paste.

Variation: To make eggplant and okra tempura, slice 1 eggplant lengthwise, then into half-circles about ½ inch thick. Remove the stem ends from a handful of okra. Dip the vegetables into the batter and transfer to the hot oil.

rolled omelet technique

The omelet is cooked in three stages, because a minimum of three layers is required, but you can make more if you like. Mix the eggs lightly, without beating, because you do not want a fluffy omelet.

Method

1. In a mixing bowl, dissolve the sugar in the dashi, soy sauce, and mirin to make a broth. Crack the eggs into a separate bowl and stir lightly. Making sure the broth is at room temperature, add the beaten egg to it, and lightly combine.

2. Heat the omelet pan until very hot, then brush with oil.

3. If you are using a large pan, pour one third of the egg mixture into the pan. If using a smaller pan, pour in one sixth. Tilt the pan backward and forward as you pour, until you have a very thin layer of egg just covering the base (top left). The egg should immediately sizzle around the edges. Cook over medium heat until the omelet is firm around the edges but soft and runny on top.

4. Using chopsticks or a spatula, carefully roll up the cooked omelet (top right), and push it to the back of the pan.

5. Brush the empty base of the pan with oil, then slightly lift the rolled egg and brush underneath it, too. Push the egg back, while continuing to keep the pan on the heat.

6. Pour another third (or sixth) of the mixture onto the empty base (center left), tilting the pan and lifting the cooked egg so that the liquid egg flows underneath (center right). Cook until almost done, as before.

7. Using the first roll of omelet as the core, roll up the second section around it (bottom left).

8. If using a large pan, repeat the process with the final third (or sixth) of the mixture. If using a small pan, repeat the process with batches of the remaining mixture, rolling each new omelet around the previously cooked one. Tip the completed roll out of the pan (bottom right) and leave to cool.

9. Cut the omelet into 2-inch pieces and serve either alone or, if preferred, sitting on an oblong of sushi rice, with a thin strip of nori wrapped around the middle.

rolled omelet

Tools	Ingredients
Mixing bowl	*For the broth*
Small bowl	1 tsp. sugar
Omelet pan	4 tbsp. dashi
Small pastry brush	2 tsp. light soy sauce
Chopsticks or wooden spatula	1 tbsp. mirin
Knife	*For the omelet*
	6 eggs
	½ tsp. salt
	oil for frying
	prepared sushi rice *(optional)*
	½ sheet nori seaweed, cut into strips about ½ inch wide and 3 inches long *(optional)*

rolled omelet

Japan's distinctive sweetened egg roll, the *tamagoyaki*, is a common sight in sushi bars. The recipe here comes from *Food of Japan* author and filmmaker shirley booth, who lived in the country for six years and studied Zen temple cooking. "If you become quite deft at this and really want to show off, you can put a sheet of nori on one of the layers as you cook," she says. "Once rolled and then cut through, it will reveal an impressive spiral effect."

Serves 4

Preparation time: 30 minutes

grilling and tabletop cooking

Given the diminutive size of most Japanese homes, large kitchens and dining rooms are rare luxuries. This restriction has given rise to a tradition of cooking at the table, bringing some of the cooking process out of the kitchen. Grilled foods have always been a winter speciality in Japan, whether as a simple domestic home barbecue or as the high drama of a *teppanyaki* restaurant.

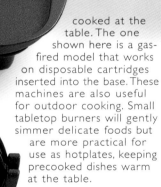

cooked at the table. The one shown here is a gas-fired model that works on disposable cartridges inserted into the base. These machines are also useful for outdoor cooking. Small tabletop burners will gently simmer delicate foods but are more practical for use as hotplates, keeping precooked dishes warm at the table.

3 Teppanyaki griddle The Japanese name derives from the Chinese word for "iron pan." This is a domestic version of the massive restaurant *teppanyaki*. Although modern in concept, it harks back to post–Iron Age Japan, when nomadic warriors cooked on makeshift iron sheets over charcoal fires. Electric or otherwise, the teppanyaki is no more than a flat iron pan for cooking at the table dishes for which minimal oil is required.

4, 5 Sukiyaki pots Sukiyaki is a sautéed dish of chicken or beef with assorted vegetables. Most Japanese homes are small and the stove is often no more than a tiny burner, so cooking on a charcoal burner or

gas ring at the dining table is expedient. There is no need for an additional utensil to serve the cooked dish because diners help themselves straight from the pot. The traditional round cast iron sukiyaki pot stands over a charcoal or gas fire, but electric versions are available.

6 Korean firepot Related to the steamboat (see page 128), firepots are also known as *sin sul lo* and come in aluminum or brass. When using the charcoal-burning type of firepot shown here, it is wise to place it on a heavy wooden trivet to prevent scorching the tabletop. Also watch out for sparks from the burning charcoal and ensure that the dining room has adequate ventilation. Electric firepots are cleaner and safer to use and have thermostat control to prevent boiling over, but lack the esthetic appeal of the traditional version.

Hibachi barbecue (*not shown*) These Japanese portable barbecues are cast iron and charcoal-fired. They have short legs so they can be set on the ground, or on a tabletop if the table is fireproof. The height above the charcoal of the grill rack can be adjusted to suit the type of food being cooked.

1 Ridged griddle This small, portable barbecue grill has a corrugated cooking surface so that grease from the food being grilled (typically meat, poultry, or fish) flows away easily. The griddle can be placed over a gas or charcoal heat source. Electric models are also available.

2 Tabletop burner This heat source is indispensable to Korean and Japanese homes. It allows dishes to be

chicken yakitori

Yakitori, bite-sized pieces of chicken threaded on skewers and grilled over charcoal, is Japan's most popular street food and a favorite bar snack. According to distinguished Japanese food writer emi kazuko, who has provided this recipe, the leg meat is most commonly used but other parts of the chicken, especially the liver, are also excellent cooked in this way.

Serves 4–8
Preparation time: 25 minutes, plus 30 minutes soaking

Tools	Ingredients	Method
12–16 bamboo skewers	6–8 chicken thighs, about	1. Soak the bamboo skewers in water for 30 minutes.
Sharp knife	1 lb., skinned and boned	2. Cut the chicken thighs into ¾-inch square pieces
Small saucepan	lemon wedges and	and thread 4 pieces onto each skewer.
Hibachi grill	powdered *sansho,* to serve	3. Combine all the ingredients for the *tare* sauce in
Basting brush	*For the tare sauce*	a small saucepan and bring to a boil, stirring. Simmer
	3 tbsp. sake	for 5 minutes, then remove from the heat.
	scant 5 tbsp. shoyu	4. Heat the grill until hot. Cook the skewered chicken
	1 tbsp. mirin	until lightly browned all over. Remove the skewers
	1 tbsp. sugar	from the heat one at a time and baste with the tare
		sauce. Return to the heat for 2 minutes to reduce
		the sauce, then remove and baste with more sauce.
		5. Repeat this process a few more times until all the
		chicken pieces are golden brown. Serve with lemon
		wedges and powdered sansho, or chili pepper.

hibachi tuna with maui onion salad

This classy dinner party recipe comes from chef roy yamaguchi of Roy's restaurants in the U.S. "If you have any leftover marinade, refrigerate it for another time," he says, "Just bring it to the boil and keep adding to it. My father had a batch that he kept going for 16 years!"

Serves 4

Preparation time: 1 hour

Tools	Ingredients
Two mixing bowls	4 tuna fillets, about 7 oz. each
	For the marinade
Saucepan	1 cup soy sauce
Hibachi grill	1 tbsp. minced garlic
Sharp knife	1 tbsp. minced ginger
Cutting board	2 scallions, sliced
	⅓ cup sugar
Wok and ladle	*For the ponzu sauce*
	2 cups sake
	2 cups mirin
	½ tsp. red pepper flakes
	4 inches kombu seaweed
	1¼ cups shoyu sauce
	juice of 3 lemons
	juice of 1 lime
	juice of 1 orange
	For the Maui onion salad
	1 large carrot
	1 small Maui onion
	1½ Japanese cucumbers, de-seeded
	½ cup Japanese spice sprouts
	8 tbsp. pickled ginger
	1 tbsp. oil
	½ cup bean sprouts
	½ tbsp. toasted white sesame seeds
	½ tbsp. black sesame seeds
	juice of 1 lemon

Method

1. Combine the marinade ingredients in a large mixing bowl and marinate the tuna for 1 hour.
2. To make the *ponzu* sauce, boil the sake, mirin, red pepper flakes, and kombu in a saucepan over a high heat for 10 minutes. Remove the pan from the heat and add the soy sauce and citrus juices. Leave the kombu in the sauce until serving time.
3. About 30 minutes or so before you are ready to serve, prepare the hibachi or a barbecue grill.
4. To make the salad, shred the carrot, thinly slice the onion, and julienne the cucumber. Combine them with the spice sprouts and pickled ginger in a mixing bowl. Heat the oil in a wok and stir-fry the bean sprouts over high heat for 15 seconds. Transfer them to the mixing bowl and toss with the vegetables.
5. Remove the tuna from the marinade and grill over a high heat for 45–60 seconds per side.
6. Divide the salad among 4 serving plates. Sprinkle with the sesame seeds and lemon juice. Place the tuna on top and spoon the ponzu sauce over the fish.

korean firepot

When there is a chill in the air, try this heart-warming dish. Electric firepots are less smoky and easier to use than those that require charcoal, however, you can keep a charcoal-burning pot warm by placing it over a fondue candle. This dish is slightly different from the "steamboats" of Southeast Asia and China in that the ingredients are all cooked together and diners then help themselves.

Serves 8–10
Preparation time: 35 minutes

Ingredients

14 oz. tender beef, thinly sliced
2 large onions, thinly sliced
6 cups beef or other meat broth
5 eggs
4 tbsp. all-purpose flour
14 oz. fish fillet, thinly sliced
¾ cup oil
5 scallions, sliced diagonally
2 carrots, julienned
3½ cups pine kernels or walnuts

Tools

Cleaver
Cutting board
Firepot
Wok and ladle
Wire mesh spoons

Method

1. If using a charcoal firepot, light the charcoal (top left) and have all the ingredients prepared (center). Put the beef, onions, and broth in the firepot and bring to a boil.
2. Meanwhile, beat 2 eggs lightly in a small bowl. Place the flour in a dish and dip the strips of fish in the egg, then into the flour to coat.
3. Heat a little oil in a wok and stir-fry the fish until cooked. Add it to the firepot.
4. Beat the remaining 3 eggs in a small bowl. Cook into an omelet in the wok, then remove and cool. Slice the omelet into thin strips.
5. Add the omelet, scallions, and carrots to the firepot. Top with the pine kernels or walnuts and simmer for 10 minutes before letting guests help themselves, each dipping into the broth with his or her own wire mesh spoon (top right) to lift out small portions of food.

small cooking tools

Japanese cuisine is known for its simplicity and minimalism. The typical Japanese kitchen is small—even cramped—by most Western standards, but Japanese cooks insist on having the right tools for each job, and quality is valued above quantity. The Japanese have a great appreciation for natural materials such as wood and bamboo, and place strong emphasis on visual appeal, so there is a synergy among the color, shape, and texture of their kitchen implements.

1 Suribachi The sturdy Japanese grinding bowl is made of high-fired pottery and scored with hundreds of tiny grooves on the inside, which act as a grater. The mortar is used with a wooden pestle to grind garlic, ginger, nuts, and seeds. The pestles come in various lengths, from 4 through 7 inches. The longer, and therefore heavier, the pestle, the better the leverage will be. To use a *suribachi*, rotate the pestle and press down, so the rounded end crushes the contents against the grooves of the bowl.

2 Square wire-mesh strainer Known as a *zaru*, this wire mesh basket is used as a straining basket for items such as noodles. Bamboo versions are also available.

3 Three-section grater This grater-cum-server is intended for small

pieces of food, especially those used as condiments, such as garlic, ginger, and daikon. It is designed to be taken to the table.

4, 5 Cooking chopsticks About 14 inches long and made of wood or bamboo, these chopsticks are indispensable in the Japanese kitchen for manipulating and turning all kinds of foods using only one hand. The length means that the cook can stay away from splattering fat while deep-frying. Some models are held together by string, others are shaped like tongs. The tips may be flat or, more usually, pointed.

6 Mandolin This curiously named and notoriously sharp implement actually looks like the musical instrument of old, though the blade is encased in tough plastic or metal. It comes with several detachable

blades that fit into the center for efficient slicing, grating, crinkle cutting, shredding, and julienne slicing. Mandolins are especially good for making paper-thin slices from tough root vegetables such as carrots and daikon. Not only Japanese vegetables benefit from the mandolin treatment: Cabbage and baby artichokes are equally well suited to fine slicing. Premium models offer better protection for the hand and are the safest to use.

7 Grater The larger teeth of this two-section grater are used for coarse grating, of daikon for instance, while ingredients such as ginger and wasabi are grated on the small teeth. These graters may be made from metal, plastic, or ceramic.

8 Metal spatula This tool is used for turning pieces of fish during cooking.

steamed snapper with soy daikon fumet

Healthy eating East-meets-West-style is the speciality of doc cheng's restaurant in Raffles Hotel, Singapore, the origin of this deliciously light recipe inspired by Japanese cooking. The original is made with the Japanese or Thai variety of snapper, but any good quality prime white fish, such as sea-bass or redfish, will do for this dish, as long as it is beautifully fresh.

Serves 4

Preparation time: 40 minutes, plus 1 hour standing

Tools	Ingredients	Method
Medium pot	4 whole small snapper or	1. To make the fumet, place the water and kombu in a pot and bring to a boil. Remove from the heat and add the bonito shavings. Set aside for 1 hour.
Grater	large fillets, about 5 oz. each	
Fine sieve	8 tbsp. oil	2. Strain the fumet, discarding the solids. Add the daikon, shoyu sauce, and shiso leaves.
Shredder	4 tbsp. sesame oil	
Cleaver	1 tbsp. finely shredded ginger	3. Season the snapper with salt and pepper and place in the steamer over boiling water. Cover and steam for 4–6 minutes over a medium heat, or until cooked.
Wire rack	2 scallions, julienned	
Small pot	salt and pepper	4. Meanwhile, gently heat the neutral-flavored oil and the sesame oil in a small saucepan.
	For the fumet	
	2 cups water	5. When the fish is done, transfer to a deep serving platter. Sprinkle with the ginger and scallions, then ladle the fumet over and around the fish.
	1 piece kombu seaweed	
	2 tbsp. bonito flakes	
	1 cup shredded daikon	6. Spoon the hot oil mixture over the ginger and scallions, and serve immediately.
	½ cup shoyu sauce	
	4 shiso leaves, finely chopped	

roast squash with cashew nut and gomasio dressing

At the Providores restaurant in London, New Zealand–born chef peter gordon prepares his trademark fusion style of cooking for an adoring, sophisticated crowd. This recipe, however, is from Peter's book on home cooking. "The most important ingredient in this relatively simple dish is the [squash], so make sure you hunt out the sweetest and tastiest there is," he advises.

Serves 4–8
Preparation time: 1 hour 30 minutes

Tools	Ingredients
Sharp knife	3 lb. 5 oz. squash, peeled and de-seeded
Cutting board	2 tbsp. sesame oil
Large ovenproof dish	1¾ cups boiling water
Suribachi	a large bunch of arugula
Mixing bowl	salt and black pepper
	2 tbsp. toasted sesame seeds
	4 tsp. sea salt flakes
	1 cup cashew nuts, toasted and finely chopped
	⅓ cup mirin
	⅓ cup lemon juice

Method

1. Preheat the oven to 375°F. Cut the squash into 8 evenly sized chunks and place them in an ovenproof dish. Lightly season with salt and pepper, sprinkle with the sesame oil, then pour in the boiling water. Roast in the top part of the oven until tender, 40–80 minutes, depending on the type of squash.
2. Meanwhile, make the dressing. Using the suribachi, grind the lightly toasted sesame seeds and sea salt together into a fine powder. Transfer to a mixing bowl and add the chopped cashew nuts, mirin, and lemon juice. Mix well and reserve until the squash is cooked.
3. Arrange the hot squash on a plate and scatter some arugula leaves on top of it. Adjust the seasoning of the dressing to taste, then pour it over the arugula, and serve.

eggplant salad with tart sesame dressing

This recipe from Tokyo-based cooking expert elizabeth andoh makes a terrific summer salad when chilled and served on crisp leaves. She says, "The same dressing, by the way, could transform the most mundane tomato and cucumber slices into an interesting Oriental salad."

Serves 2–3

Preparation time: 20 minutes

Tools	Ingredients
Knife	I eggplant, about 12 oz.
Cutting board	I tbsp. white sesame seeds
Bowl	½ tsp. sugar
Colander	I tbsp. soy sauce
Pot	I tbsp. rice vinegar
Frying pan	a pinch of salt
Suribachi	½ tbsp. water or dashi
	crisp salad leaves, to serve (optional)

Method

1. Peel the eggplant and cut it into ¼-inch-thick diagonal slices. Cut these slices into ¼-inch-thick strips and soak them in a bowl of cold water for 5–6 minutes to remove any bitterness and avoid discoloration.
2. Drain the eggplant, then blanch it in a pot of boiling salted water for 2–3 minutes. Drain the cooked eggplant strips and pat them dry to remove excess moisture.
3. In a heavy-based frying pan, dry-roast the sesame seeds. Crush them, while still warm, in the suribachi.
4. Add the remaining ingredients, one at a time, stirring and grinding after each new addition.
5. Just before serving, toss the eggplant strips in the tart sesame dressing. Serve the salad at room temperature, or chilled and arranged on crisp salad leaves if preferred.

serving dishes and lacquerware

In keeping with the insistence on serving foods that are seasonal, most Japanese homes have separate sets of dishes and utensils for each season. Each item is carefully chosen to reflect the right synergy. Lacquerware has been a part of Japanese table art for centuries, and some of it is extremely fine. In Korea, similar serving dishes are used, though some items are uniquely Korean.

1 Larger bowls Noodle soup, usually a meal in itself, is a highly enjoyable Japanese dish. The noodles and soup are typically served in large bowls such as this.

2 Soup spoon These spoons are used in Japan for dishes such as noodle soup, where the bowl is too large to be lifted to the lips.

3 Chopsticks and rest Japanese chopsticks taper to a point. Even though disposable sets are commonplace, beautifully decorated chopsticks are considered a special gift and are presented in magnificent packages. The chopstick rest is an elegant means of ensuring that the food-stained tips of the chopsticks do not touch the table.

4 Plate In Japanese cuisine, flat plates are used for many dishes, not specifically for fried rice or noodles as in Chinese service. They may be round, square, or oblong.

5 Lacquer soup bowl Japanese soups are served in these lidded lacquer bowls rather than in porcelain or pottery. The lids efficiently retain the heat and the resulting steam makes them fit tightly. Remove the lid by applying gentle pressure around the rim of the bowl. The soup inside is then sipped delicately from the bowl, as though it were a cup.

6 Rice bowl Whether made of lacquer or porcelain, Japanese rice bowls have a gentler curvature than the traditional round, squat Chinese rice bowls.

7 Condiment dishes Shape and texture are important at the Japanese table. Unlike in Chinese culture, in which sharp corners and square shapes symbolize evil and death, the Japanese do not mind using oblong and square containers. Small dishes such as these are used for serving condiments and dipping sauces.

8 Korean chopsticks and spoon Unlike the Japanese, the Koreans frequently use spoons. They also favor long, pointed chopsticks made of wood or metal.

9 Soba basket Known as a *zaru*, this square bamboo rack is specially designed for serving cold soba noodles.

10 Woven bamboo basket This small basket can serve as a napkin-holder at the dining table, or it may be used to present a single large sushi roll.

11 Bibimbap bowl This heavy stone bowl on a wooden trivet is used for serving Korea's famous *bibimbap*.

8

9

11

12

13

10

12 Bento boxes Compartmentalized lacquer boxes called bento are used to serve complete meals. With their stunning and varied designs, individual boxes and large bento sets, even the disposable models produced for lunch and snack sales on trains, are considered collectors' items. This style of bento box is used to serve food during the intermission at the theater.

13 Sushi bench Looking like a low stool of porcelain or pale wood, a sushi bench is only used to serve sushi and sashimi portions. The idea is to create a harmony of color and texture—the jewel-like colors and rich textures of raw fish against the pale, smooth bench.

14 Porcelain rice scoop Japanese rice scoops are flat and are often made of porcelain with beautiful designs. Because the country's rice is starchy, a flat scoop does the job easily and without spillage.

14

bibimbap

This is one of the most popular dishes in Korea. Bibimbap incorporates a variety of different vegetables (and sometimes meat) in a spicy sauce. It is always served over plain rice and, for panache, may be presented in this traditional heavy granite bowl mounted on a wooden trivet.

Serves 4
Preparation time: 30 minutes

Tools

Rice cooker
Mixing bowl
Pot
Cleaver
Cutting board
Wok and ladle
Bibimbap bowl
Colander

Ingredients

8 dried shiitake mushrooms
1 cup jasmine rice
1 small carrot, julienned
2 yard-long beans, julienned
⅔ cup bean sprouts
6 large leaves bok choy, sliced
2 eggs
1 tsp. black pepper
2 tbsp. gochugang sauce
1 cup ground beef
3 tbsp. sesame oil
2 tbsp. vegetable oil
⅓ cup water

Method

1. Soak the dried mushrooms in a bowl of warm water for about 20 minutes, or until soft. Meanwhile, cook the rice in the rice cooker.
2. In a large pot of boiling water, cook the carrots, beans, and bean sprouts for 5 minutes, then drain in the colander.
3. Drain and quarter the softened mushrooms.
4. Heat 2 tbsp. oil in the wok and fry the beef for 2 minutes. Add the pepper and *gochugang* sauce and stir-fry for 1 minute. Add the blanched vegetables and continue stir-frying for 2 minutes.
5. Add the bok choy and mushrooms and stir-fry for 2 minutes, then stir in the sesame oil and water. Cook for 2 minutes.
6. Place the rice in the bibimbap bowl and cover with the meat mixture.
7. Clean out the wok, and fry the eggs in 1 tbsp. oil. When cooked, place the eggs on the bibimbap and serve.

simmered sweet tofu

This is one of the many simmered dishes in Japanese cuisine, but it is often served cold, as an appetizer. It looks fabulous presented on a plain dish. The caramelized sugar gives the sauce a slightly bittersweet taste. You can use any type of tofu, including egg-flavored, for this dish.

Serves 1–2
Preparation time: 20 minutes

Tools	Ingredients
Cleaver	1 tbsp. oil
Cutting board	1 tbsp. sugar
Small pot	1¼ cups tofu
Ladle	1 tbsp. light soy sauce
	1 tsp. cornstarch
	½ cup water
	½ scallion, finely shredded

Method
1. Heat the oil in a frying pan. Add the sugar and cook just until it begins to turn color. Remove from the heat.
2. Add the soy sauce and water, then return the pan to the heat and bring to a gentle simmer.
3. Dissolve the cornstarch in 2 tbsp. water and stir it into the sauce. Cook, stirring, until it thickens.
4. Cut the tofu into cubes, add to the pan, and simmer for 1 minute.
5. Serve hot sprinkled with the scallions, or allow to cool, then chill for 1 hour to serve as a cold appetizer.

salt-grilled trout

It is fun to serve a meal, especially lunch, in bento boxes, and this salt-grilled trout recipe is an ideal dish to feature as the main ingredient. It can also be served as part of a Japanese meal, paired with daikon pickle. If fish does not take your fancy, chicken yakitori (page 61) is another good recipe for bento boxes. Serve with a mound of cold, cooked, sticky rice sprinkled with black sesame seeds, a little green salad, and some pickled ginger.

Serves 4
Preparation time: 25 minutes

Tools	Ingredients
Fish slicer	4 large trout
Cutting board	2 tbsp. fine table salt
Metal or bamboo skewers	4 heaping tbsp. daikon pickle (page 50)
Hibachi barbecue	2 tbsp. lemon juice
	oil for basting

Method

1. Gut and clean the trout, but leave it whole. Pat the fish dry and salt it liberally inside and out. Leave the salted fish to stand for 25 minutes at room temperature.
2. Using metal or bamboo skewers, pierce each trout through the head just behind the eye and across 2 inches of the lower body toward the tail. You should be able to lift the trout up by holding the end of the skewer.
3. Grill over charcoal for 6 minutes on each side, basting with a little oil during cooking to prevent dryness.
4. When the fish is done, carefully remove the skewers and place on a serving platter, or cut up for inclusion in a bento box. Drizzle lemon juice over the fish and serve with the daikon pickle.

chilled soba noodles

High summer in Japan can be oppressive, with unforgiving 110°F heat and high humidity. No surprise then, that chilled noodles are a great comfort, innocent of all but the lightest mirin dressing. This dish is traditionally served in an elegant bamboo box with a separate cup of dipping sauce that is held close to the chest while eating, to minimize splashing.

Serves 4
Preparation time: 15 minutes

Tools	Ingredients
Large pot	5 oz. soba or thin somen noodles
Small pot	1¼ cups dashi broth
Wire mesh drainer	⅔ cup mirin
	4 tbsp. shoyu sauce
	1 tbsp. sesame oil

Method

1. Bring a large pot of water to a rolling boil. Add the noodles gradually, so as not to stop the water from boiling. Stir gently to prevent sticking, and cook according to the package instructions.
2. Meanwhile, combine the dashi, mirin, and soy sauce in a small saucepan, bring to a boil, and simmer for 5 minutes. Cool the sauce quickly by holding the bottom of the pan under cold running water.
3. When the noodles are done, rinse them under cold running water and set aside to drain thoroughly.
4. To serve, sprinkle with the sesame oil and stir, then blend the noodles with a little of the cold sauce and toss well. Divide the noodles among the serving boxes and place the dipping sauce in a cup or small bowl. If desired, add a couple of ice cubes to each serving or garnish with thin strips of nori seaweed.

three simple soups

Whether breakfast, lunch, or dinner, a nourishing soup is served at every Japanese meal. Slightly cloudy miso soups, made with one of the many varieties of soybean paste, are perhaps the best known, but clear soups are also popular. All are based on dashi, Japan's ubiquitous broth, made from kombu seaweed and dried bonito flakes. Dashi is available as a convenient, powdered concentrate.

shrimp soup

Soften a small piece of *wakame* seaweed in a little cold water for 10 minutes. Trim away any tough parts, then slice the remaining wakame into ¾-inch pieces. Meanwhile, shell and devein 8 medium-size shrimp. Bring a pot of water to a boil and blanch the shrimps for 2 minutes. Drain and set aside. Blanch the wakame for 1 minute and drain under cold running water. Place the seaweed in bowl of clean, cold water to soak. Mix 3¼ cups water and 1 tbsp. dashi concentrate in a pot and bring to simmering point. Add salt to taste. To serve, place 2 shrimp and a small amount of wakame in a bowl and top with the dashi. Garnish each bowl of soup with ½ tbsp. cilantro leaves and serve hot.

miso shiru

Drain 7 oz. tofu and cut into ¾-inch cubes. In a saucepan, blend 3 tbsp. miso with 3¼ cups water and 2 tbsp. dashi concentrate, and heat until the liquid just reaches the scalding point. Add the cubed tofu and 4 tbsp. chopped scallion, and when they are piping hot, serve immediately.

clam soup

Scrub 16 clams under running water to remove the grit. Soak in a bowl of cold water for 30 minutes, then drain. Place the clams in a pot with 3¼ cups water and a 4-inch piece of kombu, and bring to a fast boil. Remove the kombu after 5 minutes and continue to cook the clams until they open. Scoop the clams out with a slotted ladle and set aside. If preferred, you can cut out the clam meat and serve it without the shells. Slice 2 celery sticks thinly and add to the broth with 2 tsp. salt, 2 tbsp. grated lemon zest, and the clams. Simmer for 3 minutes and serve immediately.

tea and sake sets

Japan's famous tea ceremonies traditionally take place in rustic teahouses, with the simplicity of the setting intended to enhance the meditative ritual of the formal ceremony. However, green tea is also the preferred beverage for everyday meals. Sake, the Japanese rice wine, can be drunk during meals, but would normally be removed from the table once the rice was served.

1 Sake set Possibly the smallest of all liquor containers, sake bottles (called *tokkuri*) are veritable works of art, often featuring beautiful designs reflecting Japanese life and culture. Some sake cups are so small as to be almost thimble-size, because sake is meant to be drunk in small amounts. This makes sense, given its potency. Deemed a drink of the Shinto gods, emperors, and shoguns, sake is Japan's oldest drink, a clear essence of boiled rice, to which yeast is added to start the fermentation process. It may be served warm or chilled.

2 Tea cups Authentic Japanese tea sets come with five cups, never four or six, because the number five is considered lucky in Japan's mysterious system of numerology. Japanese tea cups are much taller than the cups used in China. They are always made of fine porcelain or coarse pottery and are usually straight-sided. They have no handles because the cups are meant to be raised to the lips using both hands.

3 Tea whisk In the Japanese tea ceremony, bitter-tasting powdered green tea known as *matcha* is gently whipped to a froth in hot water by the tea-master who uses this delicate bamboo whisk. To the Japanese, bamboo is symbolic of longevity and reverence. Using a metal whisk is therefore completely inappropriate to the traditional ceremony, which is a calming, spiritual experience rather than a culinary one, though food is served along with the tea.

4 Teapot Japanese teapots are relatively small. Cast-iron ones such as this are expensive and generally reserved for special guests.

ice cream desserts

Green tea ice cream is a very modern concept, but it probably derived from the traditional *uji gori*, a kind of sorbet first made in the river town of Uji, south of Kyoto, which is famous for its green tea. Only *matcha* powdered green tea is used to make it. This is a modified version, produced quickly by infusing the tea in vanilla ice cream. In Japanese tempura bars, green tea ice cream is coated in special batter and deep-fried to give a popular sweet treat eaten at the end of a meal. Deep-fried ice cream is often thought to be a traditional Chinese dessert too, as it is sometimes served in Chinese restaurants in the West. In fact, it is believed to have been invented by Chinese immigrants to Australia! This easy version uses phyllo (strudel) dough, rather than tempura batter or bread crumbs, to protect the ice cream from the hot oil. The ice cream could be any flavor.

deep-fried ice cream
Place a large platter or metal tray in the freezer to chill. When it is very cold, scoop out balls of ice cream and place them on the cold platter or tray, keeping them well separated. Place in the freezer and leave until rock-hard. When ready to proceed, take 8 sheets of phyllo dough and stack them on top of each other, and cut into 6-inch squares. Heat some oil for deep-frying. Working quickly, place a portion of ice cream in the center of each square, gather up the sides, and pinch to seal into a package, wetting the edges with a brush so that they stick together and completely enclose the ice cream. Fry in the hot oil until the pastry is golden brown. Drain thoroughly and serve immediately with a caramel or chocolate sauce or dark corn or maple syrup.

green tea ice cream
Remove 1¾ cups vanilla ice cream from the freezer and allow to soften in a mixing bowl. Meanwhile, in a saucepan, bring ⅔ cup whole milk to a boil, then remove from the heat. Stir in 1 tbsp. powdered green tea and set aside to steep for 20 minutes. Blend the milky tea with the softened vanilla ice cream, beating vigorously with a wooden spoon until well incorporated. Place in a plastic lidded container and freeze for several hours before serving.

india,
pakistan,
and sri lanka

india, pakistan, and sri lanka

Cooking on the Indian subcontinent has been influenced by Greek, Mogul, and Persian invaders, spice-hungry Arab traders, and periods of British, Portuguese, and French rule. The civilization stretches back some 5,000 years. When coupled with the area's sweeping geographical differences, it is not surprising that the kitchens of India, Pakistan, and Sri Lanka boast a varied collection of culinary curiosities.

Geographically, the Indian subcontinent varies widely, from soaring mountain ranges, a dramatic coastline, and deserts, to the fertile plains of the three great river basins. The lay of the land, as well as historical, cultural, and religious differences, have produced a fascinating mix of culinary styles.

The Mogul empire fostered a rich and refined cuisine. Imports from the Middle East of dried fruit, almonds, and pistachios became integral features of royal banquets. The Parsies of India left their native Persia in the first century A.D., yet their cooking continues to reflect classic Persian flavors. Well-known Indian desserts such as *kulfi* and *gulab jamun,* also have their origins in central Asia. *Gulab* means "rose"; these sweetmeats are fried balls of curd cheese dipped in rose-scented syrup. Kulfi, India's favorite frozen dessert, takes its name from the conical mold in which it is frozen, which was brought to India via Kabul with the Moguls. Delicate rice pilaf from Lucknow and rich Hyderabad biryanis have always been made using the finest long-grain rice, combined with spiced meat, often colored with saffron, and flavored with almonds and raisins.

Popular tandoori dishes, characterized by spiced yogurt marinades, get their name from the clay oven in which the meat or fish is roasted. Tandoor ovens can be found throughout Asia and are also used for baking flatbreads, such as pita and *nan.* Although red food coloring may be the hallmark of tandoori curry houses in the West, there are no artificial additives in traditional tandoori recipes.

Whereas breads are the mainstay of the North Indian diet, the southern states use rice as the staple. South Indian cooking makes the most of local produce—coconuts, curry leaves, cashew nuts and the tart tamarind, while kitchens in northern India, such as in the state of Punjab, use a lot of dairy products, preferring to cook favorite dishes in vegetable or butter ghee (clarified butter), instead of oil. Recipes from Bengal, East India, are flavored with nutty-tasting mustard oil, and a fair share of western coastal dishes from Goa are influenced by the cuisine of the colonial Portuguese. Many dishes are surprisingly mild, depending more on the depth of spice blends than on fierce chili power. That is not to say that cooking styles across the subcontinent are known

ABOVE: **1** pistachios, **2** basmati rice, **3** chapati flour, **4** paneer, **5** cashews, **6** appam flour, **7** yogurt, **8** chickpeas, **9** green lentils. OPPOSITE: **1** corn, **2** plantain, **3** eggplant, **4** jackfruit, **5** coconut, **6** mango, **7** okra, **8** spinach, **9** curry leaves.

for their subtlety. Tribal dishes from states such as Andhra Pradesh, South India, are loaded with what locals call the *guntur,* or "flaming chili," just one bite being enough to set your mouth on fire. Contrary to popular belief, authentic Indian cooking does not always involve hours at the grinding stone. A simple fillet of fish wrapped in a banana leaf and baked with a minimum of spices can be enjoyed with as much relish as shellfish simmered in a carefully blended broth of rich coconut milk, crushed chilies, ginger, and garlic.

Indian cooks are masters at coaxing maximum flavor from humble vegetables, using deft spicing techniques and winning combinations of contrasting ingredients. Soupy, delicately spiced lentils and legumes are served at most meals. The blandness of chick-peas may be offset by the sourness of pomegranate. Split lentils are treated to tangy tamarind, and kidney beans are simmered with a gingery masala. In coastal regions such as Bengal, Kerala, and Goa, the Hindu population, which does not normally consume meat, is happy to add variety to its daily vegetables with tiny fried shrimp and red chili peppers.

Over and above geographical influences, religious beliefs play a fundamental role in the varied cooking styles of India. Hindus, for example, do not eat beef, and some communities will not touch milk or honey, either. Muslims require meat to be slaughtered by the *halal* (ritual slaughter) method, and they do not eat pork.

Kitchen duties are certainly not taken lightly. Many wealthy Brahmins, for example, feel duty-bound to preserve the purity of their high caste by ensuring that home cooking is overseen by a live-in *maharaj* (head cook), who may enter the kitchen only after

BELOW: **1** cinnamon sticks, **2** cloves, **3** turmeric powder, **4** saffron strands, **5** dried red chili peppers, **6** cardamom pods, **7** fennel seeds, **8** fenugreek seeds, **9** star anise, **10** black peppercorns, **11** coriander seeds, **12** cumin seeds.

throughout India for its sharp, homemade pickles, refined milky grain dishes flavored with saffron and cardamom, and innovative ways of cooking vegetables.

There are a great many similarities between the cooking of northwestern India and Pakistan (formerly West Pakistan, from which East Pakistan split to become Bangladesh) and in fact it can be difficult to tell them apart. Pakistan is a Muslim country. Although Islam eschews the eating of pork, the cuisine features all other meats, especially lamb, and boasts many grand dishes in the Mogul imperial tradition. Saffron pilaf, *biryani*, *samosa*, and *chapati* are as Pakistani as they are Indian. These dishes can be fiery with chilies or mild and subtle.

Much of what is perceived to be Indian cooking in the West actually hails from Bangladesh. Although separated by a distance of about 900 miles from Pakistan, it echoes with the same spicy resonance. Bangladesh was once a part of the eastern province of Bengal, and the influences are palpable. The coastline that caresses the Bay of Bengal is fecund with seafood, and the cooking tends toward briny produce, with spices used liberally. Ghee is used less often because Bangladeshi chefs tend to favor the more neutral-tasting fats, such as vegetable, mustard, and coconut oils.

Sri Lanka is the "pearl" that hangs at the tip of the Indian crown. A tiny island of undulating landscape formerly known as Ceylon, it marked a convenient halfway point between Asia's two most active trading empires. Consequently, Sri Lanka has an incredibly rich culinary heritage. The best cooking is generally based on the highland village traditions. Vegetables, fruits, and homegrown meats and poultry feature prominently, and the abundant local seafood enriches every Sri Lankan table.

Much of the cuisine is stamped with the influences of Arab, Indian, Malay, Portuguese, Dutch, and British traders and settlers. Many Sri Lankan dishes have marked Portuguese elements, such as the use of red wine vinegar and tomatoes, because these Europeans ruled Sri Lanka for about 150 years starting in the sixteenth century. Saffron-flavored rice came to the island from northwestern India. Sri Lankan rotis are also similar to the flat breads of India, and the cuisine features a mouth-watering range of seafood, beef, and poultry curries. The most famous Sri Lankan dishes are undoubtedly sweet hoppers (a type of noodle) and the spiced rice dish *lampries*, which is derived from Dutch *lomprijst*.

bathing and having said his daily prayers. Jains follow a faith closely related to Buddhism and will not cook with onions or garlic, in the belief that both ingredients increase body temperature and inflame lust. Despite the implied austerity of the phrase "pure vegetarian cooking," the Jain community is known

processing spices, herbs, and coconut

Food processors have not yet found a place in Indian kitchens, with many cooks still pledging allegiance to the large household grinding stone, and trusty mortar and pestle. The truth is that pounding ingredients extracts maximum flavor, and food processors simply do not deliver as good a result. Mixing intricate blends of dried spices is the mainstay of most Indian cooking. Contrary to what you might think, it is a quick, simple process and a joy to perform.

1 Coconut grater With this sturdy implement, pieces of coconut still in their shells can be grated simply by cranking the handle. An L-shaped metal rod is fitted through a stainless steel mount, one end featuring a crosshead with serrated edges and the other a small rubber handle. A lever attached to the rubber suction cap at the bottom of the mount forms a vacuum that secures it to any smooth surface. In South India, where fresh coconut is used daily, some households have a very large version of this contraption that incorporates a stool for sitting.

2 Herb shredder This stainless steel gadget with a handy fold-back lid is for shredding fresh herbs and aromatics. When cranked, the handle turns a sharp-toothed spindle that efficiently cuts through the ingredients inside.

3 Stone mortar and pestle Similar to that used in Southeast Asia and Indochina, this mortar and pestle are used for grinding aromatics such as garlic, onions, and chili peppers. It may be made of granite or marble and comes in various sizes.

amounts as required in useful little cup-shaped mortars such as this popular brass model.

5 Square table-shaped grater Here, tough aluminum is shaped into a miniature table, the top punctured with holes, their sharp edges facing upward to act as a grater. A plate or tray can be placed underneath to catch the shredded food.

7 Spice box India's most useful and ubiquitous kitchen tool has to be the round stainless steel spice box, a tightly lidded tin filled with smaller containers. It is used for storing essential spices and holds between five and seven smaller tins. Some have an additional layer for larger items such as cinnamon sticks.

4 Brass mortar and pestle Freshness is fundamental to spice cooking, and Indian cooks never keep ground spices for long because they lose their flavor and fragrance. Dried whole spices are ground in small

6 Individual spice tin This single stainless steel container is useful for storing large or bulky spices, such as cinnamon sticks, bay leaves, cardamom pods, and other dried fragrant ingredients.

8 Brass and wood coconut grater A slightly convex brass grater is mounted on a sturdy wood frame. The protruding teeth are effective shredders of coconut, gourds, and other tough ingredients.

indian spice pastes

Although spices play an integral role in every Indian meal, housewives in India insist on buying them in small quantities because they easily lose their distinctive aromas, especially when exposed to air and kept in hot, humid conditions. Spices may be used raw, but are frequently toasted or fried before further use. Spices should always be toasted whole and pounded afterward. Good Indian cooks are skilled at blending ingredients for spice pastes, and individual households take pride in handing family recipes down through the generations. The pastes are best made just before cooking, not in bulk, in order to maximize freshness and flavor. The following recipes demonstrate the wide range of flavors that can be achieved.

a paste for pork vindaloo

In a mortar, pound 1 small onion and 3 cloves of garlic to a paste. In a heated, dry frying pan, toast 3 dried red chili peppers, 2 tsp. cumin seeds, ¼ star anise, and a 2-inch cinnamon stick over low heat until they give off a nutty aroma, about 30 seconds. Remove from the pan and grind the spices to a powder before blending them with the onion and garlic. Heat 2 tbsp. oil in a karahi and fry the mixture over a low heat, stirring for 4 minutes, or until oil comes to the surface. Add 1 tsp. salt, 2 tbsp. vinegar, and 5 tbsp. water. Stir over a low heat until the paste (bottom left) thickens. It is now ready for the next step of cooking.

Add 1 tbsp. grated ginger and grind until well incorporated with the chili peppers. In a small mixing bowl, combine 2 tbsp. minced onion, 1 tbsp. ground coriander, 2 tsp. ground cumin, 2 tsp. ground turmeric, and ½ tsp. ground cinnamon with 1 tbsp. tamarind juice, to make a paste. Stir in 8 fresh curry leaves, 4 whole cardamoms, 2 tsp. salt, and the pounded chili and ginger paste. To use, heat 4 tbsp. oil in a karahi and gently fry the spice paste, stirring continuously, over a low heat for about 5 minutes, or until the mixture is fragrant.

a paste for goan fish curry

To make a paste (bottom right) for 1¾ lb. fish, soak 5 dried chili peppers in a little water to soften. In a mortar, grind 1 tbsp. coriander seeds and 1 tsp. cumin seeds. Add 1 tbsp. paprika and ½ tsp. turmeric powder, and blend well. Remove the spices from the mortar and replace with chili peppers. Add 1 large onion, 3 cloves garlic, and 1 tbsp. grated ginger. Add the spice mix, 1 tsp. salt, and 3 tbsp. water. To use, heat 4 tbsp. oil and fry the paste over low heat for 4 minutes before adding the fish.

a paste for grilled chicken

This paste (top right) is for rubbing into 4 skinned chicken joints (legs or breasts) for broiling. Grind 1 tbsp. grated ginger and 3 cloves garlic until fine. Add ½ tsp. pounded black peppercorns and 1 tsp. chili powder. Heat 1 tbsp. ghee in a karahi, and fry the paste over a low heat for 4 minutes. Add 1 tsp. salt, 1 tsp. sugar, and 1 tbsp. lemon juice. Remove from the heat, cool, then rub the paste over the chicken.

a paste for mutton curry

To make a curry paste (top left) for 1¾ lb. cubed lamb or mutton, soak 6 dried chili peppers in a little warm water until soft, then pound them to a paste.

okra thoran

Thorans, an essential part of Keralan meals, are dishes of crunchy stir-fried vegetables flavored with coconut and curry leaves. das sreedharan of Rasa Restaurants says his favorite school lunch was a tiffin of rice, yogurt, pickled vegetables, and a thoran dish such as this one. Any combination of crunchy vegetables can be substituted for the okra, known as *bhindi* in India.

Serves 4
Preparation time: 20 minutes

Tools	Ingredients
Small knife	1¾ cups okra
Cutting board	5 tbsp. oil
Karahi	1½ tbsp. mustard seeds
Colander	10 curry leaves
	2 dried red chilies
	1 onion, finely chopped
	1 tsp. turmeric powder
	⅔ cup freshly grated or desiccated coconut
	salt

Method

1. Chop the okra into ½-inch pieces and set aside.
2. Heat the oil in a karahi and add the mustard seeds. As they begin to pop, add the curry leaves and chilies, then the finely chopped onion.
3. Cook, stirring, for 5 minutes until the onion softens, then stir in the turmeric powder and a little salt and stir-fry for 2 minutes. Add the chopped okra and cook 3–4 minutes.
4. Remove the pan from the heat and add the coconut. Mix well, then serve hot.

pots, pans, and griddles

An Indian kitchen is designed to stand up to the toughest of tasks. Catering for extended families calls for cavernous karahis and enormous pots, called *patilas*, that are often large enough to feed a family of fourteen in one sitting. It is best to choose pans that are made from heavy-gauge

1 Karahi pan Also known as a *kadai* or *cheena chatti*, this utensil is not very different in shape from the Chinese wok, but most karahis are smaller in size. In India, they usually have a rounded base; however, most karahis available in the West have flat bottoms that enable them to sit flat on electric burners. They usually have two handles and are made of cast iron, aluminum, enamel, or stainless steel. The enamel karahi shown here is effectively a nonstick pan that can be scrubbed without fear of scratching the surface. When the handles are made of the same metal as the bowl section, they can get quite hot while on the stove and therefore care must be taken in moving the pan. The karahi is used for sautéing spices and pastes and making vegetable dishes, as well as for deep-frying.

2 Small karahi These small karahis, a familiar sight in restaurants, can be brought directly to the table.

3 Tawa One of the most important utensils in the Indian kitchen is a cast iron griddle that often has a long handle. Tawas are used for cooking breads such as parathas and chapatis. In South India, they are used for frying *dosas*, pancakes made from ground rice and lentils. Tawas are a good conductors of heat and cook breads evenly without scorching. They are also ideal utensils for roasting spices. Tawas come in many sizes. The smaller

ones are no larger than 4 inches in diameter, but others may be the size of a bicycle wheel!

4 Black terra-cotta curry pot Traditional vessels used throughout the subcontinent for thousands of years, terra-cotta or clay pots often have thick rims and are used for simmering curries and stews on charcoal-burning braziers. The model shown here is matte black with the patina of age, having been

metal, and in India such equipment is often sold by weight. A light pan cannot hope to hold its own against the often complicated stages of frying and scraping spice pastes. Most homes in India use gas burners, which suits the rounded bases of many patilas, tawas, and karahis. A considerable amount of heat would be lost if these tools were used on an electric stove. Listed below are common cooking utensils found in kitchens across the subcontinent.

handed down through several generations of the owner's family.

5 Straight-sided aluminum pot Known as a patila in India, this is an all-purpose pot for rice and curries. Care must be taken not to cook dishes of an acidic nature in this type of pot because the aluminum will react with the food. It has no handles and comes with a flat, tight-fitting lid.

6 Stainless steel pot Many cooks are fond of using stainless steel pots because they are durable and easy to clean. This round-bottomed stew pot with a copper base tapers toward the lip and is used for curries and boiling liquids.

7 Stainless steel yogurt maker Yogurt is a staple food in homes across the subcontinent, and most cooks make their own on a daily basis, using a teaspoon of the previous day's yogurt to set a new batch. Stainless steel yogurt makers are more durable

than their terra-cotta counterparts, and are available in many sizes.

8 Terra-cotta yogurt maker Terra-cotta crocks are thought to be the best for setting yogurt because they give a superior texture and the porous clay helps to keep the yogurt cool during the hot summer.

9 Idli pan *Idli* are the staple breakfast dish of South India. These are made from a fermented mixture of rice

and lentil flour and are steamed. The mixture is cooked in a stainless steel or aluminum steamer that resembles a large egg poacher. This round-bottomed steamer has two decks (some have as many as four) containing molds for four idli on each layer. The molds are fixed to a central rod and the idli cooked in the steam produced by the simmering water in the bottom part of the pan. The rod allows for easy lifting and removal of the cakes.

roast chicken madurai masala

Madurai, a town in the South Indian state of Tamil Nadu, is noted for its mild dishes, of which this chicken recipe is typical. It comes from top chef cyrus todiwala of London's Café Spice Namaste. Although the list of ingredients is long, the dish is very simple to make.

Serves 4

Preparation time: 1 hour

Tools	Ingredients
Knife	4 chicken thighs, with skin
Cutting board	2 tsp. salt
Lidded pot	½ tsp. turmeric powder
Basting spoon	3 tbsp. oil
	10 curry leaves
	½ tsp. cumin seeds
	½ tsp. fennel seeds
	3 bay leaves
	4 medium onions, finely sliced
	1 tbsp. ginger paste
	1 tbsp. garlic paste
	3 medium tomatoes, halved
	1 tsp. coriander powder
	½ tsp. chili powder
	1 tbsp. chopped cilantro
	10 mint leaves, shredded

Method

1. Clean the chicken thighs, removing any excess fat. Rub with salt and turmeric powder and set aside.
2. Heat the oil in a pot and add the curry leaves, cumin, and fennel seeds. Fry until brown, shaking the pan vigorously to prevent burning.
3. Add the bay leaves and onions, and sauté until the onions are light brown. Add the ginger and garlic pastes and cook, stirring, for 1 minute. Then add the tomatoes and continue to cook until almost dry.
4. Mix the coriander and chili powders with a little water to make a paste and add it to the pan. Cook for 1 minute while stirring, then push the fried paste aside.
5. Lay the chicken thighs in the pan, skin-side down and spread the paste over them, rubbing it in well.
6. Cover, reduce the heat, and brown the chicken pieces on the skin side. Add 2 tbsp. water to create steam and facilitate the cooking.
7. Turn the chicken thighs over and continue cooking for 15 minutes or until done. To test if cooked, pierce the thickest part of one thigh with a metal skewer. If the liquid that runs out is clear, the chicken is ready.
8. Add the cilantro and mint leaves, cover the pan, and remove from the heat. Serve immediately.

fruit-flavored lassi

More than just a drink, Indian *lassi* is a real coolant, a yogurt beverage similar to a milkshake, and the best way to quell the fire of a hot, spicy curry. Plain versions come salted or sweet, with a hint of cardamom, but fruit-flavored lassi is increasingly popular. If you prefer not to make your own yogurt, choose a mild live yogurt, which is good for the digestive system. Most Indian stores sell puréed mango, and whole jackfruit and lychees canned in their own juice are usually available in Asian food stores.

To make enough mango, jackfruit, or lychee lassi for four people, you will need at least 1½ lb. of canned fruit in its own juice. Reserve a few small pieces of fruit to use as a garnish, then purée the rest with the juice from the can. In a large mixing bowl, beat 2 cups plain yogurt until creamy, then blend in the fruit purée. Chill thoroughly. To serve, pour into tall glasses, add a little crushed ice, and garnish with the reserved fruit. For a tangy variation common in southern India, use buttermilk in place of the yogurt.

spiced lamb with almonds

Not all Indian dishes call for hours at the grinding stone, yet even the simplest recipes can produce dramatic flavors, says Indian television chef roopa gulati. Simple, dry dishes like this one have their origins in the desert, where water and fresh vegetables are hard to find.

Serves 4

Preparation time: 1 hour

Tools	Ingredients
Knife	1¼ lb. boneless leg of lamb, cut into ¾-inch cubes
Cutting board	
Lidded pot	7 oz. plain yogurt
Small karahi	3 onions, finely sliced
Spoon	4 garlic cloves, finely sliced
	¾ inch ginger, thinly sliced
	¾ inch stick cinnamon
	2 small bay leaves
	3 cloves
	¼ tsp. black peppercorns
	1 tsp. cumin seeds
	6 tbsp. oil
	1 blade mace
	2 dried red chili peppers, split and de-seeded
	4 tbsp. flaked almonds
	2 tbsp. cilantro leaves
	a few drops of pandanus leaf (screw pine) essence *(optional)*

Method

1. In a pot, combine the lamb, yogurt, 2 of the sliced onions, the garlic, ginger, cinnamon, bay leaves, cloves, peppercorns, cumin seeds, and 4 tbsp. oil. Mix well, add a little salt, and bring to a simmer. Cover tightly, reduce the heat, and cook gently for about 40 minutes, or until the meat is tender.

2. Once the meat is cooked, heat the remaining 2 tbsp. oil in a small karahi and add the rest of the sliced onion, plus the mace and red chili peppers. Reduce the heat and gently fry the onions until they are very soft in texture and a nutty golden color.

3. Stir the onion mixture and flaked almonds into the meat. Season to taste with salt, and reheat the lamb as necessary. Sprinkle with the cilantro leaves and a little pandanus leaf (screw pine) essence, if desired, just before serving.

bread-making implements

Many centuries ago, the Moguls brought fine-textured breads to the subcontinent, and royal kingdoms took pride in the skill of their cooks. The best bakers are considered to be the Muslims, and after years of making flaky breads, they have adapted their skills well to rolling out puff pastry and croissant doughs. Even in the rice-eating areas of India, most homes have a rolling pin and chapati board lying next to the flour-bin, and the culinary skills of prospective brides are often judged by the standard of bread-making.

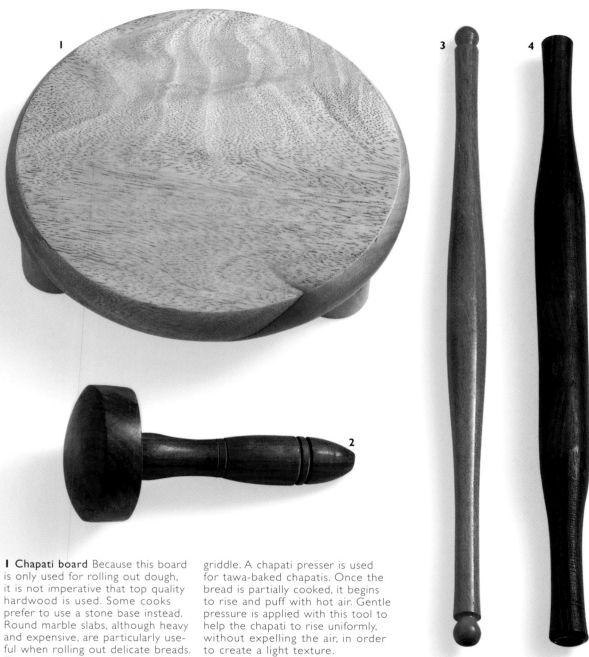

1 Chapati board Because this board is only used for rolling out dough, it is not imperative that top quality hardwood is used. Some cooks prefer to use a stone base instead. Round marble slabs, although heavy and expensive, are particularly useful when rolling out delicate breads. The cool marble surface is oiled to keep rich doughs from sticking during the hot summer months.

2 Chapati presser There are two types of chapati, one baked in a tandoor, the other on a tawa or griddle. A chapati presser is used for tawa-baked chapatis. Once the bread is partially cooked, it begins to rise and puff with hot air. Gentle pressure is applied with this tool to help the chapati to rise uniformly, without expelling the air, in order to create a light texture.

3, 4 Chapati rolling pins Rolling pins are usually made from hardwood and are narrow, with tapered ends. Chapati boards and rolling pins can be found as sets in Indian stores and street bazaars.

paratha

There are many different types of paratha, some as simple as a dough made from whole wheat flour and water, enriched with oil or ghee. It is primarily the way the dough is worked that distinguishes this bread from other popular flatbreads, such as chapati.

Serves 8

Preparation time: 40 minutes

Tools	Ingredients
Mixing bowls	⅔ cup ghee, plus extra for greasing
Chapati board	4 cups all-purpose flour
Rolling pin	2 tsp. sugar
Tawa pan	1 tsp. baking powder
Brush	2 eggs
	1 cup milk or water
	a dash of salt

Method

1. Melt the ghee and mix with the flour, sugar, baking powder, and salt. Lightly beat the eggs and milk and add them to the bowl.

2. Knead for at least 10 minutes, or until a soft dough forms. Wrap dough in a damp towel and allow to stand for at least 2 hours.

3. Divide the dough into 8 portions and shape into balls. While you work with one, keep the others covered with a damp cloth.

4. Flatten the ball (top picture) and roll out into a thin circle on lightly floured board. Fold over once to make a half moon (left center), then again to make a curved-edge triangle (below left). Roll out again until twice the size and dust with a little flour.

5. Fold all the edges inward to make a rough circle again, and roll out for the last time into a circle about ¼ inch thick.

6. Heat the tawa and grease with a little ghee. Place the paratha on it and cook until bubbles appear. Flip over and cook the other side (bottom picture), brushing the bread with a little more melted ghee. When done, the paratha should be golden brown.

nan bread

An authentic nan needs to be cooked in an authentic tandoor. The technique involves rolling out the dough, opening the lid of the tandoor, and slapping the bread onto the wall of the oven, where it will stick. This recipe from menernosh mody of London's Franco-Indian restaurant La Porte des Indes should give good results with a domestic oven.

Serves 14
Preparation time: 40 minutes, plus 2 hours rising

Tools
Sifter
Large bowl
Rolling pin
Tawa
Baking trays

Ingredients
4 cups all-purpose flour
1 tbsp. baking powder
1 tsp. sugar
1 egg, lightly beaten
1¼ cups milk, boiled and cooled to lukewarm
1¼ cups lukewarm water
4 tbsp. oil
2 tbsp. sesame seeds
melted butter, for brushing
a pinch of salt

Method
1. Sift the flour into a large bowl with the baking powder, sugar, and salt. Make a well in the center and gradually add the egg, milk, and water. Stir to blend the ingredients into a dough.
2. On a floured surface, knead the dough until firm. Return the dough to the bowl, cover with a warm, damp cloth, and leave to rise for 30 minutes.
3. Knead the oil into the risen dough, then leave to rise again, covered with a warm, damp cloth, for 1 hour or until the dough has doubled in size.
4. Punch the dough down. Divide into 14 balls of equal size and place them on a floured tray.

Cover once again with a warm, damp cloth, and leave to rise for 30 minutes.
5. Heat the oven to 475°F and place 2 cookie sheets in it to heat. On a lightly floured surface, roll out each ball into a teardrop shape ¼ inch thick. Sprinkle with sesame seeds.
6. Grease the hot cookie sheets, and, working in batches, place the nan on them. Bake for 5–6 minutes, or until golden brown and puffed. Brush with melted butter before serving.

molds and presses

India is a nation of munchers, where crunchy snacks are distinguished by their varied shapes and textures. Many tools for snack-making have remained unchanged for thousands of years, and people are often surprised that the complex spirals of spicy bites such as *murukku* have been created by a simple-looking press. *Kulfi* molds were originally made of clay, and in many old quarters of the subcontinent, these traditional ices continue to be frozen in the same clay pots today.

3 Kulfi molds These cone-shaped molds with screwtop lids are used for making kulfi, India's famous frozen dessert. Aluminum is a popular material for molds because it cools more quickly than plastic when placed in ice. Traditionally, kulfis were made in clay pots sealed with dough.

1 Seviya press This little brass cylinder with a crank handle incorporates a selection of perforated plates, each with small holes, or gashes, chosen according to the shape of snacks required. The press is used for making Sri Lankan string hoppers, South Indian murukkus, and other sweet and savory snacks. The dough is pressed into the cylinder, then the top lid of the press is wound down into place. When the handle is turned, it pushes the dough out in the desired shape, ready for steaming or deep-frying.

4 Vadai maker Vadais are round, savory rice-flour cakes that look like exotic donuts. They originate from South India, but are popular throughout the country. The plunger on this stainless steel gadget forces the vadai dough out in a ring that is ready for frying.

2 Stainless steel ricer In the West, this tool is most commonly used for ricing cooked potatoes. In South India and Sri Lanka, ricers are sometimes used to shape string hoppers. The ricer is made of stainless steel and has a hinged lid that presses the dough through the perforated base when force is applied. This is done over oiled plates or banana leaves, so that the piles of string hoppers created are ready for steaming.

string hoppers

Indian *appam* (*idiappam* in South India), Sri Lankan *appe*, and string hoppers are from the same family. Basic recipes vary with regional differences, but rice flour and coconut milk are the main ingredients. A batter is forced through holes in a metal mold into a tangle of thin threads, which are steamed before serving. Most Indian and Sri Lankan stores sell appam flour ready mixed for cooking.

Serves 4

Preparation time: 35 minutes

Tools	Ingredients
Mixing bowl	1½ cups appam flour
Ladle	⅔ cup coconut milk
Steamer	½ tsp. salt
Seviya mold	fine brown sugar for sprinkling
Plate	oil, for greasing

Method

1. Sift the appam flour into a bowl and pour in the coconut milk and salt. Beat to a smooth batter with a creamy consistency.
2. Meanwhile, bring water to a boil in a steamer and place a lightly oiled plate in the pan. Cover tightly and allow the steam to build up.
3. To make the string hoppers, use a seviya mold fitted with a perforated disk that has notches the diameter of matchsticks cut out of it. Pour the appam batter into the mold.
4. Rotate the handle of the seviya mold over the plate in the steamer, making small mounds of appam threads. Repeat until there are enough piles to fill the plate, making sure that the sides do not touch.
5. Cover and steam for 10–15 minutes, or until the hoppers are fluffy and fragrant. Transfer to a serving platter and sprinkle with the sugar before serving hot.

saffron and cardamom kulfi

A favorite Indian dessert, kulfi is an ice cream traditionally made by reducing the milk over a gentle heat for a very long time. However, it is also easy to make with evaporated milk. This recipe comes from camellia panjabi, who is one of India's most respected restauranteurs and cooking writers, as well as a director of England's prestigious Group Chutney Mary.

Serves 4

Preparation time: 45 minutes, plus freezing time

Tools	Ingredients
Kulfi molds	4 tbsp. sugar
Small pot	3 cardamom pods
Wooden spoon	2 15-oz. cans evaporated milk
Cleaver	12 saffron strands
	3 tbsp. heavy cream
	2 silver foil leaves, to decorate
	(optional)

Method

1. Add the sugar and cardamom pods to the milk in a heavy-based saucepan and cook over low heat for 10 minutes, stirring and scraping the sides and bottom of the pan continuously.

2. Remove the pan from the heat and discard the cardamom pods before adding the saffron. Mix well and leave to cool before stirring in the cream.

3. Fill the kulfi molds, cover, and freeze for 4–5 hours.

4. To remove the kulfi from the molds, dip each one into hot water, and press out the ice cream. Decorate with silver leaf, especially for festive occasions.

small cooking tools

Implements used in an Indian kitchen are rarely chosen for their good looks. Cooks are far more concerned with durability and lay little emphasis on decoration. Because many of the tools pictured below are handcrafted, quality and appearance vary with each piece. Street markets are the best places to buy such equipment at affordable prices.

1 Long-handled scoop This long wooden scoop is ideal for stirring gravies and pouring soupy lentils into small dishes. As is done in Southeast Asia, empty coconut shell halves are used as ladles in South India and, like this model, have a stick attached that acts as the handle.

2, 3 Large wooden masher Cooked vegetables such as spinach, eggplant, and potato are often mashed with this fearsome-looking wooden tool. The club-shaped head is usually grooved along the sides, which also makes it useful for churning yogurt drinks such as lassi and for making homemade butter.

4, 5 Wooden spatulas This flat wooden tool is a versatile addition to the kitchen and may be used in the same manner as wooden spoons.

6 Steel spatula This thin, flat spatula is useful for turning fried eggs and flipping delicate dosas.

7 Steel service spoon Some Indian chefs favor these comparatively flat spoons for cooking curries.

8 Tongs Because many cooking pots do not have handles, tongs are often used to remove *patilas* from the stove. They are also an invaluable tool for turning chapatis while they cook on a griddle.

9 Round winnowing basket of woven palm leaves In rural India, rice and other grains are winnowed after harvesting, to separate the chaff from the grain. Small amounts are placed in the basket (or a flat tray of similar materials) and lightly tossed in the air.

10 Tandoori skewer Tandoori meats are marinated and skewered on this long metal spear before roasting in special tandoori ovens. Such skewers require deft handling and turning, hence their length and weight.

11 Sieves This set of four different-size mesh grids is used for sifting flours and other powders. In India, chapati flour is always sieved before use.

tiffins and serving items

Bombay is famous for its tiffin (luncheon). After vegetables and curries have been cooked, lunches are carried in tightly lidded stacked tins to offices across the city. When it comes to tableware, stainless steel is preferred to china or aluminum. Although relatively expensive, steel has a lengthy lifespan and does not react to the acid in tangy Indian pickles.

1 Tiffin carriers The term "tiffin" was coined by the British when they ruled India and was used to denote a light midday meal that may have included shepherd's pie and trifle for dessert. Today, tiffin boxes are a stacked tower of stainless steel containers filled with homemade chapatis or rice, lentils, vegetable curry, and perhaps a meat dish. Tiffin deliveries in Bombay have grown into a lucrative business. After lunches have been made at home, meals are collected by tiffin boys who then deliver thousands of hot meals to offices throughout the city. So successful is the industry that the delivery boys have formed their own trade union.

2, 3 Lunch boxes Many school students take these small boxes to school because they are just the right size to hold a mid-morning snack. They often have built-in trays for pickles and relishes. Although plastic boxes are gaining in popularity, steel boxes continue to be chosen for their durability.

4 Thali and katori sets At Indian meals, different dishes are served together on a *thali* (steel tray) in *katori* (separate bowls). Katoris come in many sizes and are used for serving individual portions of lentils, curries, candies, and yogurt. Ceremonial thalis may be ornately decorated and made of copper or silver, but everyday versions are usually stainless steel or aluminum.

5 Pickle server These stainless steel sets with tiny accompanying spoons are a familiar sight in curry houses, where they are used for serving pickles and sauces. In India, dry spices such as toasted cumin and pounded chili peppers, for sprinkling over dishes, may also be served in them.

6, 7 Rice scoops Found in all Indian homes, these metal scoops are used for serving rice at the table.

palak paneer

Most homes in India make their own *paneer* (soft cheese) by adding enough vinegar to boiling milk to separate the curds from the whey. The curds are then pressed for about 30 minutes, or longer if a firmer texture is preferred, to give a nutritious form of protein that is important to India's many vegetarians. In the West, ready-made paneer is now available in many supermarkets. This recipe comes from yogesh arora of the Tiffin Room at Raffles Hotel in Singapore.

Serves 4

Preparation time: 10 minutes

Tools	Ingredients	Method
Knife	2 tbsp. oil	**1.** Heat the oil in a saucepan and sauté the onion and garlic until golden brown. Add the chopped ginger and green chili and cook for 2 minutes more.
Cutting board	1 small onion, minced	
Karahi	1 tsp. minced garlic	**2.** Add the spinach, then the butter, cream, pepper, ground cardamom, garam masala, and salt.
Spatula	1 tsp. minced ginger	
	1 large green chili, chopped	**3.** Mix in the paneer and stir over moderate heat for about 2 minutes, until the cheese is heated through. Adjust the seasoning to taste and serve immediately.
	6 cups chopped spinach leaves	
	2 tbsp. butter	
	2 tbsp. light cream	
	¼ tsp. white pepper	
	a pinch of ground cardamom	
	a pinch of garam masala	
	7 oz. paneer, cubed	
	a pinch of salt	

lamb samosas

Perhaps the best-known Pakistani and Indian snack, samosas are sold everywhere in the streets. They may contain a variety of meat and vegetarian fillings and lend themselves to experimentation. Asian grocery stores sell ready-made samosa wrappers, though phyllo and strudel dough are acceptable substitutes. Tiny samosas make great cocktail snacks.

Serves 8
Preparation time: 45 minutes

Tools

Small knife
Cutting board
Small pot
Colander
Karahi
Plate
Spoon
Wire mesh ladle

Ingredients

14 oz. samosa wrappers
oil for deep-frying
For the filling
5 oz. potatoes
5 oz. mutton curry paste
  (see page 82)
14 oz. lamb mince

Method

1. To make the meat filling, peel the potatoes and cut into ½-inch cubes. Bring a pan of water to a boil and cook the potatoes for 10 minutes. Drain well and set aside in a bowl to cool.

2. Heat the curry paste in the karahi and stir in the ground lamb. Cook for 10–20 minutes over a low heat, then add the cooked potatoes. Stir for another 2 minutes and transfer to a plate to cool.

3. To shape the samosas, place a spoonful of meat mixture in the middle of one end of a pastry strip (above left). Dampen the edges with a little water to help seal them. Fold a corner of the pastry over the mixture to form a triangle (above center), then continue folding in alternate directions to make a triangular package (above right).

4. Heat some oil for deep-frying in the karahi and deep-fry the samosas until golden brown. Remove with a wire mesh ladle or slotted spoon and place on a paper towel to drain. Serve hot.

indochina

including thailand, vietnam, laos, myanmar, and kampuchea

indochina
including thailand, vietnam, laos, myanmar, and kampuchea

The Buddhist culture of Indochina has Hindu roots and dates back 3,000 years to the days when India began trading with China after the Silk and Spice Roads opened. With the inevitable intermarriages of Indian, Chinese, and local peoples, the resulting culinary mix has become an endearing blend of hot, sweet, sour, aromatic, and savory flavors—often all in one dish.

For Thai cooking in particular, the keynote is the artful blend of fresh herbs and other aromatics, which are often ground to a paste and cooked in a little oil before being combined with coconut milk, tamarind juice, or broth. In addition to the well-known green and red curries that evolved from early Indian influences into uniquely light concoctions, typical dishes of Thailand include satay, fish and shrimp cakes, delicious soups, and salads zesty with lime and lemongrass. When it comes to presentation, the Thais are masters at transforming fruits and vegetables into glorious works of sculptured, edible art.

Kampuchean or Khmer cuisine echoes Chinese and Thai elements and, like Laotian cooking, tends to rely on glutinous rice. The Mekong River that runs through the region yields abundant fish and shellfish, and these, along with vegetables, are the key ingredients, augmented by free-range chicken, duck, pigeon, and tiny paddy-field birds. Pork and beef are rarely used. Lamb is hardly ever seen outside the cities and is eaten almost exclusively by tourists. At every Kampuchean meal, there is a pungent dip of chili peppers and fish sauce. Noodle dishes are the staple fare of the rural folk to which fish, chicken, game, and spices are added. Wild mushrooms and jungle greens turn up in salads, and coconut milk is the basis for simple desserts made from bananas, mangoes, and the many other tropical fruits.

The cornerstone of Myanmar meals is perfectly fluffy rice accompanied by a variety of pickles and dips. A typical family meal will consist of rice, a hot-and-sour soup, fish and chicken curries, cellophane noodles, salads of leaves and indigenous greens, and always a dip of *balauchaung*, made from chili peppers, lime juice, shrimp paste, and dried shrimp. Many of the region's dishes require little cooking; raw salads and pickles predominate.

The cuisine of Vietnam, a country that was once a French colony, is a curious amalgam of Chinese, Thai, and French cooking, with rice and rice

noodles as the staple, though French baguettes are often served with stir-fried dishes! The Vietnamese fish sauce, called *nuoc mam*, is more pungent than the Thai version. The country's famous beef soups are richly aromatic with Chinese five-spice blends, but it is the noodles that truly mark Vietnamese cuisine. They feature in *pho*, the definitive beef noodle

ABOVE: **1** rice paper wrappers, **2** black rice, **3** coconut milk, **4** fish sauce, **5** shrimp paste, **6** peanuts, **7** dried shrimp, **8** rice noodles, **9** palm sugar. OPPOSITE: **1** galangal, **2** Thai mango, **3** lemongrass, **4** cilantro, **5** holy basil, **6** red chili peppers, **7** coconut, **8** limes, **9** Thai eggplant, **10** lime leaves, **11** bird's eye chilies.

dish, which includes a broth perfumed with cinnamon, coriander, pepper, and other spices. Like the Thai people, the Vietnamese are fond of salads, but these are certainly not boring plates of lettuce leaves. Cabbage, carrots, celery, fruits, and steamed chicken, for example, will be tossed in aromatic dressings of sesame oil, lime juice, and sugar, and strewn lavishly with mint, cilantro, and chilies to produce wonderfully vibrant, pungent dishes.

natural leaves and containers

In many parts of Asia, the local plant life is put to ingenious use as wrappers, skewers, plates, containers, and other natural utensils. These "tools" are fundamental to the rustic flavor of the cuisines. A wonderfully sustainable resource, they play the dual role of being functional while

1 Banana leaves As large as umbrellas, subtly perfumed, and extremely pliable, banana leaves are excellent for wrapping large items of food, usually whole fish for steaming, braising, and grilling. They are thick enough to use as disposable plates and are used widely as such in India and Southeast Asia, as well as in Indochina. Specialty stores sell them trimmed and folded and they need only a quick rinse in hot water before use. Store them away from cold air or they will turn yellow and brittle within a few days.

2 Pineapple halves Thai chefs are particularly adept at finding new functions for this succulent tropical fruit, using the flesh as an ingredient and the shell as a highly fragrant serving dish. The remaining half of the shell is used as a lid to keep the food warm during the meal. The natural juices still in the fruit enhance the dish in a magical way.

3 Lemongrass These grass-like plants have a heady and pervasive scent, especially at the root end. They are generally about ½ inch thick but when really lush, can grow to twice this girth. The thin 6-inch long leaves are usually discarded. Whole stems make natural lemon-scented skewers around which ground meats and seafood can be wrapped. When bruised and shredded at the root end, lemongrass becomes a basting brush with natural citrus flavor. The plant's thick roots can be split and stuffed with ground food before grilling. The lower 1½ inches or so of the root end is typically ground with other spices and herbs to make curry pastes.

4 Squash shells In Thailand, small squashes weighing about 2¼ lb. are hollowed out and filled with a mixture of egg, coconut milk, and sugar, then baked until golden brown. The squash meat is rendered soft and sweet, an ideal companion to the coconut-and-egg custard. Larger squashes can be sliced into wedges and filled in the same way. The Indonesians use squashes as receptacles for fruity curries.

5 Pandanus leaves Measuring about 14 inches in length, these dark green aromatic leaves (sometimes called screw pine or kewra) have a distinctive vanilla scent.

imparting subtle fragrances to the food. With so many Western countries now home to burgeoning Asian immigrant communities, the demand for these hitherto rare items is being met by air shipments. These rough-and-ready tools have been used long before metal was first mined.

When blanched and trimmed into even strips, they can be folded and shaped into little cups to hold coconut and rice-flour puddings. Large pieces are wrapped around spiced chicken and shrimp for deep-frying. Small bits are placed on the surface of rice and curries to give a subtle aroma. They will keep for about two weeks in the crisper section of the refrigerator. In India, pandanus leaves are used to make a fragrant water that is added to dishes at the end of the cooking time to impart a heady fragrance.

6 Bamboo leaves Often sold dried, bamboo leaves are about 10 inches long and 3 inches wide at the center, tapering to a point at both ends. Traditionally used as wrappers for triangular rice dumplings, in commemoration of a Chinese poet, they impart an aroma not unlike that of dried corn husks. The dried leaves keep well for months but must be soaked in hot water before use to make them pliable.

lemongrass shrimp satay

Lemongrass is used as an herb throughout Southeast Asia, but here it is ingeniously employed as a skewer. You don't actually eat the lemongrass stalk because it is too fibrous, but the citrus tang it imparts to the barbecued ground shrimp paste is delicious.

Serves 4

Preparation time: 40 minutes

Tools	Ingredients	Method
Cleaver	1 lb. fresh raw shrimp, shelled and deveined	1. Chop the shrimp with the cleaver and set aside.
Mortar and pestle	3 scallions	2. Using the mortar and pestle, grind the scallions, chili peppers, and garlic until very fine. Add the shrimp and continue to grind until the mixture resembles a paste.
Mixing bowl	3 fresh red chili peppers	
Large spoon	2 cloves garlic	
Charcoal brazier	2 eggs	3. Transfer the paste to a mixing bowl and add the eggs, lime juice, fish sauce, cornstarch, pepper, and sugar. Mix well, kneading until the mixture is thick and doughlike in consistency.
	juice of 2 limes	
	2 tbsp. fish sauce	
	1 tbsp. cornstarch	
	1 tsp. black pepper	4. Take about 2 tablespoons of the mixture and shape it around a lemongrass stalk. Repeat with the remaining mixture and lemongrass stalks until all are used. Brush lightly with vegetable oil.
	1 tsp. sugar	
	10–12 lemongrass stalks, about 5 inches long	
	2 tbsp. oil	5. Heat a charcoal brazier or broiler and cook the satays for 5–8 minutes, turning frequently until the shrimp mixture is slightly charred. Serve warm.

fish steamed in banana leaf

Before cooking, this Myanmar dish may be appear to be simply a spicy fish paste mixture, but the result is more than the sum of its parts—an intoxicating blend of fish, meat, spices, and fragrant herbs. During steaming, the mixture inside the leaves sets to become firm and sliceable.

Serves 6
Preparation time: 25 minutes

Tools

Cleaver
Cutting board
Mortar and pestle
Banana leaves
Large spoon
Small bamboo skewers
Bamboo steamer

Ingredients

3 lime leaves, very finely sliced
1 small bunch of basil leaves, sliced
2 tsp. salt
1 tsp. sugar
1¾ lb. fish fillets
3 eggs, lightly beaten
2 tbsp. oil
1 tbsp. cornstarch
1 cup thick coconut milk
For the spice paste
3 medium onions
8 candlenuts
12 dried chilies, soaked until soft
2 tbsp. ground coriander
1 tbsp. shrimp paste
3 slices galangal
2 stalks lemongrass

Method

1. Grind all the ingredients for the spice paste in a mortar until smooth, then mix with the lime leaves, basil leaves, salt, and sugar.
2. Grind the fish coarsely and mix with beaten egg, oil, cornstarch, and spice paste. Knead briefly and gradually add coconut milk, stirring until you get a buttery consistency.
3. Scald the banana leaves in boiling water and drain. Cut into pieces measuring 11 x 9 inches. Place 2 tablespoons of fish on the banana leaf.
4. Fold up the sides so that the fish paste is enclosed in the leaf. With the thumb and forefinger, press one end to form two straight edges, about 4 inches from the end (bottom left).
5. Do the same with other side, making a package with folded edges overlapping and flush with the top edge of the long side. Secure firmly with a bamboo skewer (bottom right).
6. Place in a bamboo steamer and steam for 15 minutes. Open the banana leaf package and slice the paste—which will have set—into bite-size slices or cubes before serving.

pineapple fried rice

The Blue Elephant restaurants, tropical hothouses of orchids and other heady blooms, are known as much for their evocative ambience as well as for their quintessentially Thai menu. Use the largest pineapple you can find for this recipe based on the royal fried rice of chef chang, whose grandmother was a lady-in-waiting at the Court of the King of Thailand. His original dish uses a rather complex sauce, for which a bouillon cube has been substituted here.

Serves 2
Preparation time: 35 minutes

Tools	Ingredients
Rice cooker	1 fresh pineapple
Cleaver	1 cup Thai fragrant rice
Small all-purpose knife	4 tbsp. vegetable oil
Cutting board	2 large eggs
Spoon	4 tbsp. mixed bell peppers,
Wok and ladle	finely diced
	2 tbsp. minced onion
	2 tbsp. diced carrot
	4 tbsp. cooked shrimp
	4 tbsp. crabmeat
	1 tsp. salt
	½ tsp. white pepper
	½ tsp. sugar
	1 fish or vegetable broth cube,
	dissolved in 2 tbsp. water
	2 scallions, finely sliced
	2 tbsp. chopped cucumber
	2 tbsp. chopped tomato

Method

1. Cook the rice in the rice cooker. Drain and allow to cool overnight in the refrigerator.

2. Cut the pineapple in half lengthwise with a cleaver. With a small knife, cut deep into the sides of each half, about ½ inch in from the skin. Cut all around the fruit and down through the core, keeping a ½ inch away from the skin. Make small crosswise cuts and lift out chunks of pineapple flesh. With a spoon, scoop out the remaining pieces, leaving a smooth, oval-shaped container.

3. Loosen the cold cooked rice grains with a fork. Heat the oil in the wok until very hot. Break the eggs into the wok and scramble them. Add the rice and stir-fry for 2 minutes.

4. Add the peppers, onion, carrot, shrimp, and crabmeat, and continue stir-frying for 1 minute. Add the seasonings, sugar, and broth, and mix well. Toss in the scallions, stir, and remove from the heat.

5. Carefully transfer the fried rice mixture to the pineapple shells and sprinkle with the chopped cucumber and tomato before serving.

bamboo leaf dumplings

Originating in China, these dumplings have become staple snack fare throughout Indochina, each region and food vendor having its own spicy filling. Dried bamboo leaves are sold in all Asian grocery stores and have to be blanched in boiling water before use to make them pliable.

Serves 4

Preparation time: 2 hours, plus overnight soaking for rice

Tools	Ingredients	Method
Cleaver	14 oz. lean pork	**1.** Cut the pork into ½-inch cubes and place in a pot of boiling water for 1–2 minutes to blanch. Drain.
Cutting board	3 tbsp. minced onion	**2.** In a mortar, grind the onion and garlic to a paste. Heat the oil in the wok and fry the paste for 4 minutes. Add the pork and stir-fry for 2 minutes.
Small pot	2 tbsp. minced garlic	
Colander	2 tbsp. oil	
Mortar and pestle	2 tbsp. ground coriander	**3.** Add the coriander, ground cumin, sugar, and salt, and cook for 2 minutes. Add the water and cook over high heat until the mixture is almost dry but still moist. Transfer to a plate to cool.
Wok and ladle	1 tbsp. ground cumin	
Dried bamboo leaves	1 tbsp. sugar	
String	2 tsp. salt	**4.** Blanch the bamboo leaves in a pot of boiling water, then drain. Drain the soaked glutinous rice.
Large pot	1 cup water	
Wooden tongs	1¾ cups glutinous rice, soaked overnight	**5.** Fold one leaf in half, making a triangular container with a long back from two leaf ends. Place 1 tbsp. rice on the bamboo leaf, press on 1 tbsp. of the pork mixture, and cover with another 1 tbsp. rice. Fold over both leaf ends to make a pyramid-shaped dumpling.

6. Hold the dumpling firmly while wrapping a piece of string twice around it, and tie firmly. Leave a tail of at least 8 inches of string to make it easier to remove the cooked dumplings with tongs.

7. Bring a large pot of water to a boil, add the dumplings, and simmer for 1 hour. To serve, cut the string on the dumplings, so the diners can unwrap the leaves at the table.

grinding implements

These mortar and pestle sets are not different merely for esthetic reasons; each has specific purposes. Indochina's uniquely shaped terra-cotta version is meant for grinding delicate fresh herbs and spices for salad-making. The stronger granite version is used for pounding pungent curry pastes from firm fresh ingredients such as candlenuts, galangal, garlic, and chili peppers.

1 Terra-cotta mortar and pestle The pestle accompanying the tall terra-cotta mortar is a large wooden club about 12 inches long. It gently pounds rather than grinds foods, so is not effective for grinding tough ingredients to a paste or powder. Its depth and size, however, mean that after a salad dressing has been made in it, the other salad ingredients can be tossed and turned there too, without the need for a salad bowl. Wash in hot soapy water, then turn upside down and leave to dry before storing. Used properly, one of these will last several lifetimes.

2 Granite mortar and pestle A granite mortar can withstand the heavy pounding needed to produce fine fresh curry pastes. To use it, prepare all the ingredients and place them in individual bowls, ensuring the foods are dry to the touch. Start with drier items, such as candlenuts and garlic, before moving on to those that will splatter. Always grind a small amount at a time. With a regular thumping and circular motion, grind the spices on the bottom and sides of the mortar. Keep a spoon handy to scrape down the bits that rise up the sides of the mortar and, when done, use the spoon to scrape up every bit of paste.

green curry with fish dumplings and eggplant

Tools
Cleaver
Cutting board
Mortar and pestle
Large bowl
Pot
Wire mesh strainer
Saucepan
Spoon

Ingredients

For the fish dumplings
3 cilantro roots, scraped and chopped
a pinch of salt
1 tbsp. chopped wild ginger (*grachai*)
5 white peppercorns
7 oz. pike or monkfish fillets
2 tbsp. fish sauce or light soy sauce
½ tsp. palm sugar
1 stalk lemongrass, crushed

For the curry
2 cups coconut cream
3 tbsp. green curry paste
2 tbsp. chicken broth or extra coconut milk
fish sauce, to taste
chili peppers, to taste
2 cups coconut milk
3–4 Thai eggplants, quartered
2 kaffir lime leaves
a few long green and red chili peppers, de-seeded and julienned
a handful of Thai basil
a little shredded wild ginger (*grachai*)

Method

1. To make the fish dumplings, pound the cilantro roots in the mortar with salt, wild ginger, and peppercorns until fine in texture. Transfer to a large bowl and clean out the mortar.

2. Place the fish in the mortar and pound until smooth. Add it to the bowl and work the mixture into a ball. Pick up the ball and throw it back into the bowl. Repeat several times to develop the flavor and firm up the flesh. Season with fish sauce or light soy sauce and the palm sugar.

3. Roll and pinch portions of the fish mixture between your fingers to make dumplings about 1 inch in diameter. Bring a pot of salted water to a boil and add the crushed lemongrass. Reduce the heat, and, working in batches if necessary, gently poach the dumplings for about 2 minutes. Drain and reserve.

4. Meanwhile, in a saucepan, bring the coconut cream to a boil and cook until it separates. Reduce the heat to medium and add the green curry paste. Cook for 4 minutes, adding some chicken broth if necessary, until the curry looks like scrambled eggs. Add the fish sauce and chili peppers to taste.

5. Stir in the coconut milk and return to a boil. Add the eggplant and cook 3 minutes. Just before serving, add the fish dumplings, kaffir lime leaves, green and red chilies, Thai basil, and wild ginger.

spicy salads

Luscious ripe papayas are often thought of as a sweet fruit, but in Asia papayas are frequently used when green or unripe in savory dishes such as salads and curries, in which case they are treated as a vegetable. The green papaya salad from Thailand featured here is known as *som tam* and is made almost entirely in a large terra-cotta mortar. Below it is a raw fish salad from Kampuchea. This is also an intriguing dish, very similar to the South American ceviche, although its origins probably go back to China where raw fish was, and still is, eaten to symbolize rebirth. In Mandarin, the words for raw fish are "yu sang" which sound exactly like the term for "rebirth," but are written differently in the Mandarin script. You could also use shrimp for this dish; whatever seafood you do use, make sure it is absolutely fresh.

green papaya salad

Soak 1 tbsp. dried shrimp in a little water until soft, then drain. In a large mortar, grind 2 green chilies and 4 garlic cloves, then add the softened shrimp. Peel 1 large green papaya and shred it directly into the mortar. Melt 1 tbsp. palm sugar and add to the mortar with 2 tbsp. fish sauce and 2 tbsp. lime juice. Add 2 tbsp. chopped or torn cilantro leaves and 12 halved cherry tomatoes. Toss the salad lightly before serving.

kampuchean raw fish salad
Wash 1 lb. 5 oz. fresh tuna or salmon fillet and pat completely dry with a paper towel before cutting into chunks. Place in a mixing bowl, sprinkle with the juice of 6 limes, stir well, and refrigerate for 2 hours. In a mortar, grind 4 garlic cloves, 6 shallots, 3 slices fresh ginger, 2 stalks lemongrass, and 4 green chilies. Dissolve 1 tbsp. palm sugar in 2 tbsp. hot water and add to the mortar with 1 tbsp. fish sauce and 2 tbsp. finely shredded sweet basil. To serve, toss the marinated fish with the dressing and garnish with more sweet basil leaves.

thai curry pastes

The principles behind the preparation of Indochinese spice pastes remain constant—only the ingredients vary. These pastes, the basis of all curries and spicy side dishes, are ground to the required consistency in a granite mortar with a granite pestle. Unlike an electric food processor, this rustic tool can be manipulated at will for coarse, fine, or smooth pastes. Grinding by hand naturally takes longer, but it gives a curry of deliciously toothsome quality and allows the cook to adjust the quantities of ingredients according to their fragrance.

red curry paste
Soak 10 dried chilies in a little warm water until soft. Meanwhile, dry fry 2 tbsp. coriander seeds and 1 tsp. cumin seeds in a pan over a low heat, stirring continuously until fragrant. In a mortar, grind 1 tsp. black peppercorns, 1 tbsp. shrimp paste, the drained chilies, 1 large sliced onion, 4 garlic cloves, 2 stalks lemongrass, 1 tbsp. chopped galangal, 4 lime leaves, and 1 tsp. salt. Heat ⅔ cup oil in a wok and fry the paste over low heat for 10 minutes, stirring continuously. When the oil seeps out, transfer the paste to a bowl to cool, then store in a closed jar in the refrigerator.

green curry paste
In a mortar, grind 4 green chilies, 3 tbsp. chopped cilantro (including roots, stalks, and leaves), 2 slices galangal, 2 stalks lemongrass, 1 tbsp. shrimp paste, 3 lime leaves, 1 tsp. black peppercorns, 1 sliced large onion, 4 cloves garlic, and 6 candlenuts. Grind until fine, then stir in 1 tsp. salt. Heat ⅔ cup oil in a wok and fry the paste over low heat for 10 minutes, stirring continuously. When the oil seeps out, transfer the paste to a bowl to cool, then store in a closed jar in the refrigerator.

muslim curry paste
Dry fry 2 tbsp. coriander powder, 1 tbsp. cumin powder, 1 tsp. turmeric powder and 1 tbsp. chili powder in a pan over a low heat for 1 minute, taking care not to let them burn. In a mortar, grind 1 large sliced onion, 4 garlic cloves, 4 slices galangal, and 1 tbsp. shrimp paste. Mix in the toasted spices. Heat ⅔ cup oil in a wok and fry the paste, stirring continuously, over low heat for 10 minutes. When the oil seeps out, transfer to a bowl to cool, then store in a closed jar in the refrigerator.

green curry with fish dumplings and eggplant

Having first come to prominence at his former Sydney restaurant, Darley Street Thai, david thompson is today recognized by the Thai government as one of the world's leading experts on Royal Thai cuisine. His knowledge is manifest in his menu at the restaurant Nahm in London's Halkin Hotel, where this mouthwatering dish is featured. You can use an oily fish to make the dumplings, but will need to adjust the flavor balance of the sauce.

Serves 4
Preparation time: 30 minutes

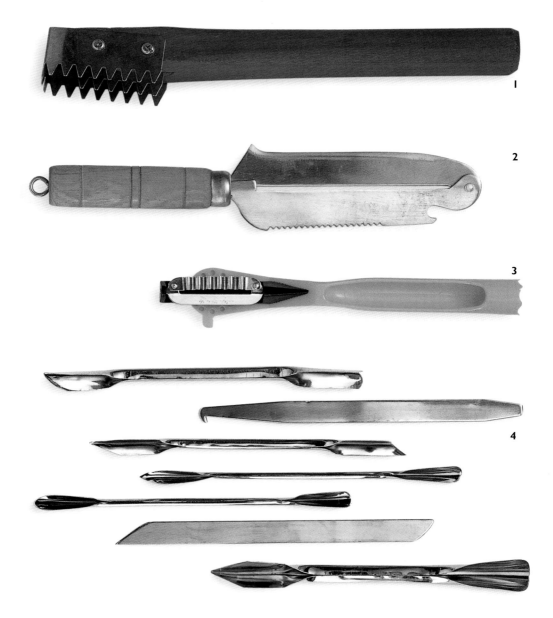

scaling, shredding, and carving

Many small jobs in the Indochinese kitchens are not small in importance because the way an ingredient is prepared has a major impact on the texture and presentation of a dish. This is most evident in Thai cooking, where salads may be given an artful touch by shredding or carving the ingredients, so that the dish looks and tastes glorious. Good cooks also prefer to do their own processing of fresh seafood, and this is performed using specific tools to make the job much easier.

1 Fish scaler This simple but effective tool comprises a wooden handle attached at one end to a serrated metal blade bent into a U-shape. The sharp teeth make short work of fish scales.

2 Dual-purpose slicer and shredder Mounted on a wooden handle, this tool makes a fine job of cutting wafer-thin slices of firm fruits and vegetables, while the serrated edge is used for producing fine shreds.

3 Vegetable shredder Suitable for right- or left-handed cooks, this swivel-bladed gadget makes fine strands of fruits and vegetables, as well as very thin slices.

4 Fruit and vegetable carving set Looking rather like a tool kit for dentists or surgeons, this collection of specialized blades is available in various sizes in Thai stores. Once the preserve of the royal kitchens, carving fruit and vegetables into intricate floral shapes is a skill of which Thai chefs are particularly proud, and the results of their labors often adorn lavish buffet tables. The tips of these tools may be curved, or pointed to near-needle sharpness for making the necessary nicks in melons and root vegetables and mimicking the delicate petals of a flower. Dexterity is enhanced by holding the tools close to the blade while carving. The sharp ends may be poked into a cork for safety when not in use.

shaped cutters and molds

The special molds and other tools for making the bewildering range of Indochinese sweetmeats, snacks, and candies have evolved over centuries. Originally made from natural materials such as wood or bamboo, they are today available in light metals. Many are shaped to echo the symbolism of which Asian cultures are so fond or designed to make intricate patterns of great beauty.

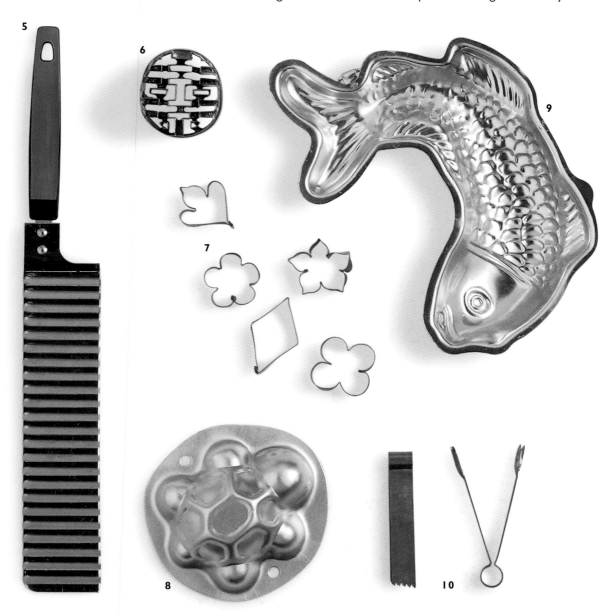

5 Long serrated cutter The gelatin desserts eaten in Indochina are not of the wobbly type known in the West. Most are firm and made from agar-agar, a seaweed by-product. In Asia, agar-agar is usually sold in long translucent strips, but in the West it is available in granules. Agar-agar has the advantage of being able to set without refrigeration, a real benefit in hot climates. Often enriched with coconut cream, the gelatin desserts are unmolded but rarely served whole. They may be cut into diamonds or triangles with a regular knife; however, this serrated cutter produces slices of gelatin that are then served from a plate.

6 Vegetable cutters Metal cutters such as these, shaped into Chinese characters, flowers, or animals, are used to stamp out shapes from slices of carrot, radish, and other hard root vegetables. The shapes are then used to decorate dishes of noodles and salads. These cutters are also commonly used in China.

7 Brass shaped cutters Strips of brass are bent into floral or heraldic cutters for little rice-flour cookies.

8, 9 Turtle and fish molds Animals, birds, and plants all have their place in ritualistic practices. These molds are probably derived from those used by European colonists in earlier times but are now used extensively in Indochina to make a wide range of desserts.

10 Tweezers Even the smallest rice-flour cake will be lovingly designed and crimped to take on pretty floral forms. These tweezers, available in several sizes, are for pinching designs and attractive crimped edges on cakes, cookies, and pastries.

vietnamese cabbage salad

This is a crisp, refreshing salad that goes well with barbecued meats or Vietnamese spring rolls, or it can be served as an appetizer. The recipe is from marlena spieler, who has written many best-selling cookbooks and is the European food correspondent for the *San Francisco Chronicle*.

Serves 8–10

Preparation time: 25 minutes, plus 30 minutes sweating

Tools	Ingredients
Cleaver	1 head white cabbage
Cutting board	1 cucumber
Mandolin	2 carrots
Dual-purpose slicer/shredder	1 bunch scallions
Vegetable shredder	5 cloves garlic
Large bowl	1–2 tbsp. shredded or chopped ginger
Large sieve or colander	6 tbsp. sugar
	3 tbsp. white wine vinegar
	juice of 2 limes or lemons
	2–3 tbsp. sesame oil
	½ tsp. dried red pepper flakes or ½ chopped fresh chili
	2 tsp. light soy sauce or fish sauce
	3 tbsp. chopped cilantro
	1 tbsp. chopped fresh mint *(optional)*
	6–8 tbsp. skinned peanuts, coarsely chopped
	a pinch of salt

Method

1. Core and thinly slice the cabbage, using the mandolin or cleaver. Julienne the cucumber, and shred the carrots. Thinly slice the scallions and chop the garlic.
2. In a large bowl, combine the cabbage, cucumber, carrots, scallions, garlic, and ginger, and sprinkle with salt. Set aside for at least 30 minutes to sweat, then drain and squeeze out the excess liquid, in handfuls at a time.
3. Add all the remaining ingredients. Taste for seasoning, then cover and refrigerate until ready to serve.
4. Before serving, drain the salad again and adjust the seasonings to taste. Serve garnished with the peanuts.

grill racks

Grilled and barbecued foods figure prominently in Indochina. Everywhere in the cities and towns from Bangkok to Ho Chi Minh City, street vendors ply their wares from makeshift carts that contain no more than a charcoal brazier and various implements for grilling meats and seafood. Racks such as these hold the food tightly yet openly, allowing the cook to baste the food liberally with marinade using a brush or a bruised stalk of lemongrass, which will add its own delicious flavor.

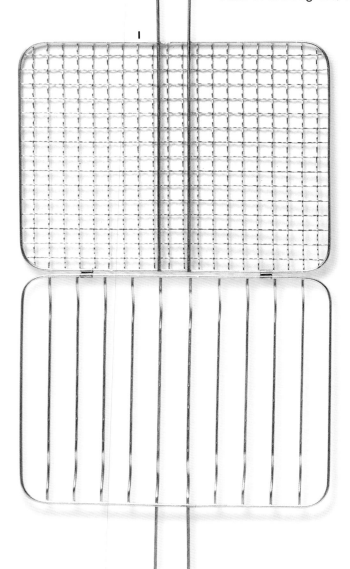

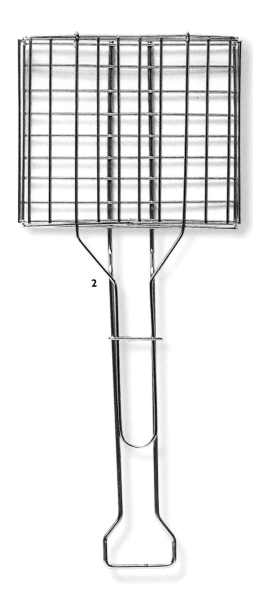

1 Large wire rack These wire racks are a modern take on the rustic bamboo versions and can hold a whole fish, chicken, or game bird, large squid, and butterflied jumbo shrimp. The handles allow frequent turning for effective barbecuing, but because they are made of metal, they get extremely hot during cooking, so it is advisable to wrap a damp towel around them. After use, scrub the racks vigorously to remove stuck-on bits of charred food and stubborn stains.

2 Small wire rack This is for grilling smaller items, such as spiced patties and shellfish, and helps to prevent flavorings such as garlic, onions, and herbs from dropping out.

north vietnamese fish kabobs

There was once a road in Hanoi called Phõ hàng chà cá, named in celebration of this dish, *cha ca nuong*, but now it has another name. This recipe from seafood expert and food historian **alan davidson** is still among the most celebrated in North Vietnam. You can use any sea fish with firm flesh, and for authenticity use *nuoc mam*, the Vietnamese fish sauce.

Serves 4

Preparation time: 20 minutes, plus 2–3 hours marinating

Tools	Ingredients	Method
Cleaver	1¼ lb. fish flesh	**1.** Clean the fish, remove any bones, and skin and cut the flesh into 1-inch cubes.
Cutting board	4 slices fat bacon	
Large bowl	3 tbsp. oil	**2.** In a large bowl, combine the ingredients for the marinade and add the cubed fish. Turn gently to coat. Let marinate for 2–3 hours.
Bamboo skewers	2 scallions, chopped	
Wok	5–6 tbsp. peanuts, skinned	**3.** Cut the bacon into 1-inch squares. Thread the skewers with alternate pieces of fish and bacon.
Small bowl	*For the marinade*	
Grill rack	3 tbsp. oil	**4.** Heat the oil in the wok and fry the scallions until soft. Transfer to a small bowl and set aside.
Basting brush	3 tbsp. fish sauce	
Mortar and pestle	2 tbsp. rice wine	**5.** Heat the barbecue. Place the skewers on the grill rack, close, and place on the barbecue. Baste the fish during cooking with the onion marinade.
	a pinch of turmeric	
	2 tsp. chopped wild ginger	**6.** Pound the nuts in the mortar and sprinkle them over the fish kabobs just before serving.
	2 tsp. shrimp paste	

coconut wood tools

The coconut palm provides more than just food in the tropics. Its leaves and trunk are used in construction, the hair covering the mature shells is made into matting, and the oil is used in cosmetics. Coconut shells are never without purpose in Asia, and even without being crafted into utensils, they make handy water scoops, all-purpose containers, and serving bowls.

1, 5 Coconut shell ladles The natural curve of coconut shells makes them ideal ladles when a handle is attached. Similar tools are found in most coconut-growing regions, including South India. The long-handled ladles are ideal for serving soups and curries, whereas shorter ones can be used as rice scoops or for serving salads and desserts.

2 Perforated spoon Coconut palm may seem rustic, yet this humble material can be shaped, perforated or carved to function like any modern kitchen implement. This one is a useful straining or draining tool.

3 Spatula This tool is finely honed to work just as well as the modern equivalent for flipping and stirring.

4 Slotted spoon Like the perforated spoon, this tool is useful for lifting sauced foods from the wok.

6 Salad servers Salads are a key feature of Indochinese cuisines. Here, fine craftsmanship transforms the coconut shell into a salad set, comprising a large fork and spoon with smooth, rounded handles.

natural basketware

Various types of palm frond are dried and woven into a range of functional and decorative containers for food storage and presentation in Indochina. Thai and Laotian cuisine, in particular, often feature sticky rice that is served in these small baskets. They do double duty as containers for rice crackers, shrimp wafers, spiced nuts, and raw vegetables.

1 Large storage basket Made of very fine bamboo weave, these baskets are square at the bottom and round at the top. This type of basket is traditionally used for storing dry grain. This is not advisable in kitchens today, because grain products should be stored in robust sealed containers to deter pests.

2 Water bucket In remote areas where modern plastic products are a rarity, large dried leaves are fashioned into buckets such as this one used for collecting fresh water.

4 Steaming basket Here, a large palm basket with sloping sides sits over a metal pot. Portions of food, usually rice, are placed in the basket, the pan is filled with water, then the whole device is set over a heat source. A separate cover is placed on top so that the food cooks in the steam generated in the base.

5 Small round basket Almost a replica of the Chinese rice bowl, this very fine weave basket is used for serving condiments, raw vegetables, and dry snacks.

3 Lidded basket A clever design featuring broad bands of bamboo interwoven with finer strips, this attractive basket has a lid attached by a string and stands securely on its integral crossbar feet. In Indochina, a basket such as this would be used for serving cooked rice.

6, 7 Small lidded baskets A tiny variation of the taller lidded basket shown at left, these are used in Thailand for serving small snacks. The baskets may be plain or decoratively woven like the star-shaped box above, with lids entirely separate or attached by a small cord.

southeast asia
including singapore,
malaysia, and indonesia

southeast asia
including singapore, malaysia, and indonesia

Not only are the three countries that make up Southeast Asia geographical neighbors, but they also share many cultural ties. Southeast Asian cooking is a heady mix of spicy, aromatic, and soy-based concoctions, liberally tweaked by cross-cultural fusion elements.

Malaysia, the Indonesian Archipelago, and Singapore evolved from an ancient Sri Vijaya Hindu empire centuries before it was sacked and overtaken by the jungle, and well before Dutch and English colonialists first laid eyes on their spice-rich promise. All three regions of Southeast Asia are places of agricultural and culinary richness, with many dishes in common.

The cuisine is a mixture of Indian, Chinese, Arab, Dutch, British, and Thai influences, with tantalizing fragrances permeating the very air. Keynote flavors include ginger, lemongrass, galangal, shallots, chilies, cilantro, coconut, tamarind, and the many fresh herbs that impart their delicious perfumes to Southeast Asia's multitude of tasty curries and stir-fries.

Fish and shellfish are spiced with chilies, turmeric, ginger, and coconut milk and steamed in banana leaves. Chicken, beef, and pork are cooked in heady blends of shrimp paste, shallots, galangal, lime leaves, and lemongrass. Skewers of marinated chicken are grilled over charcoal, rice is drenched with coconut milk and fragrant pandanus leaves. Tapioca is grated, puréed, then baked with sweet palm syrup. Delicate, wafer-thin rolls of egg and coconut batter are shaped by iron plates with intricate motifs. An endless array of spicy, savory, or sweet noodles are consumed with relish. Most of these dishes are still made in the traditional way with the tools featured in this chapter.

It is not the general practice to serve desserts after Southeast Asian meals. Many of the region's sweet specialties were originally reserved for Taoist or Buddhist rituals or to symbolize good things within the Chinese cultural pantheon. Some have over the years become popular snacks sold throughout the year, regardless of ritual links or symbolism.

The region's mixed tapestry of culinary styles is a direct result of multicultural marriages over the centuries. In particular the combination of spices, local produce, and ethnic Chinese cuisine has evolved to give a distinctive style known as Nyonya cooking. The word *Nyonya* is an amalgam of "neo," which means "lady" in Chinese, and "hya," which means "gentleman-brother"; the Malay term for

the community is *Peranakan,* which means "born of the soil," as opposed to being born in China.

Also unique to Southeast Asia is the style of street food known as hawker cooking. Indian, Malay, Chinese, Arab, and Eurasian dishes are displayed daily on the streets of every city, town, and village by itinerant food vendors. These people are a much-loved feature of the region, many working from nothing more than makeshift carts, booths, and even baskets slung on poles hoisted on sturdy shoulders. But today, with urbanization, many are relegated to covered complexes, where the authentic flavors still

ABOVE: **1** fried tofu, **2** tempeh, **3** black rice, **4** yellow bean paste, **5** shrimp paste, **6** fish balls, **7** sambal, **8** coconut milk, **9** chili sauce, **10** fish cake, **11** dried whitebait. OPPOSITE: **1** chive flowers, **2** laksa leaves, **3** galangal, **4** red onion, **5** kasturi limes, **6** gai lan, **7** red chilies, **8** garlic, **9** lemongrass, **10** pandanus leaf.

abound, even if the ambience is devoid of rustic charm. Food culture is fundamental to Southeast Asia, so the culinary heritage is kept alive and remains just as delicious, even if it is not eaten outdoors. Even in the West, dim sum restaurants serve this delicious street food at lunchtime.

street hawker tools

Despite the rapid urbanization of many Southeast Asian cities, street hawkers remain a fascinating feature, sometimes with several family members working at the same booth. Noodles, satay, fritters, pastries, black sticky rice, coconut milk mush, fresh fruit cocktails, and intriguing packages of banana and pandanus leaves are among the typical fare.

1 Woven pandanus leaf fan An enduring sight in Southeast Asian streets is the mobile satay man. Given that he never knows when he will have his next customer, his charcoal brazier always has a ready glow. This fan, fashioned from an entire dried pandanus leaf, sparks the embers of the brazier into roaring life in a few seconds. Given the humid climate and nature of his job, it is also used to cool the cook!

2, 6 Short-handled strainers These are used for quick blanching in small or shallow pans for delicate foods

such as seafood and thinly sliced meats. Each requires a certain amount of dexterity, with a twist of the wrist, to blanch, shake, drain, and turn out the food into a bowl.

3, 4 Noodle strainers Before metal and plastic became the basic materials for strainers in Southeast Asia, bamboo was the mainstay. Many street hawkers in rural areas still use the implements of old, whereas others prefer modern wire models. Long handles are practical and safest for blanching noodles in deep pots of scalding, bubbling water.

5 Perforated ladle This handy tool is for scooping froth and pieces of blanched food from pots.

7 Bamboo skewers Usually between 6 and 8 inches long, these sharp bamboo skewers are used to spear small pieces of meat or seafood for grilling. It is advisable to soak them in cold water before use to minimize scorching on the grill. In Indonesia and Malaysia, larger bamboo stakes are fashioned into gripping forks that hold a whole bird for grilling. Small slivers are also used to secure leaf containers during cooking.

fried vermicelli xiamen-style

Xiamen-style indicates that this crisp noodle dish is in the manner of those from the eastern province of Fujian in China. A key characteristic is to combine seafood and meat or chicken in the same dish. This version comes from hong sai choi of the Furama Hotel, Singapore.

Serves 2–4

Preparation time: 30 minutes

Tools	Ingredients	Method

Tools
Cleaver
Cutting board
Small pot
Bamboo strainer
2 woks
Wok ladle
Wire strainer

Ingredients
⅔ cup bean sprouts
oil for deep-frying
4 oz. rice vermicelli noodles
6 oz. chicken breast fillet, thinly sliced
½ cup raw shrimp, deveined
1 large green bell pepper, sliced
1 large red bell pepper, sliced
1 chicken broth cube
½ tsp. oyster sauce
a pinch of sugar
½ tsp. sesame oil

Method
1. In a pot of boiling water, blanch the bean sprouts for 1 minute, then drain and set aside.
2. In a wok, heat the oil for deep-frying until smoking, and fry the vermicelli a handful at a time until golden and puffed. Lift out with a wire strainer and set aside.
3. Remove all but 2 tbsp. of oil from the wok. Stir-fry the chicken and shrimp in it for 3 minutes until cooked. Remove and reserve.
4. Stir-fry the bell peppers for 1 minute, then add the chicken, shrimp, bean sprouts, broth cube, oyster sauce, sugar, and sesame oil. Stir-fry for 1 minute.
5. Briefly reheat the vermicelli in a separate wok for 1 minute, Spoon the sauce over it and serve.

tools for edible baskets

Asian chefs have always been on the cutting edge when it comes to presentation skills. With ingenuity being the mother of invention, many "plates" at banquets and other festive occasions are actually edible containers made using the special tools featured here. Such tricks are not restricted to professional chefs. In Southeast Asia, few home kitchens are without the pietee maker, which looks like a miniature golf putter, and housewives are adept at creating diminutive cups of pastry or "top hats" to be filled with all manner of cooked ingredients.

1 Pietee maker This tool comprises a heavy brass knob with smooth grooves, attached to an L-shaped metal bar. The knob is dipped into a pan of boiling oil and then into batter, to be returned to the oil to deep-fry into little baskets. When done to a crisp, the baskets come away easily from the mold. The resulting cups are shaped exactly like little top hats, then filled with cooked bamboo shoots and other fillings and served as appetizers or canapés called *kueh pietee* in the local

dialect. The story goes that they were little finger food items for parties, hence the patois translation of "pietee." In Southeast Asia the term *kueh* refers to all kinds of cakes, snacks, and candies. You need practice to make perfect cups, and if the temperature is not right, you end up with bottomless cups! However, the advantage is that you can make the cups way ahead of serving time and store them in an airtight container for up to a month. Never wash these pietee molds with detergents, because the soapy suds may linger in the joint between the knob and the bar. Just wipe clean with a kitchen towel and store in a cool, dry place.

2 Lompang mold Also known as a flower mold, this Indonesian tool features a flower-shaped ring attached to a thin metal rod. It is dipped in a sweet batter of rice flour, sugar, and coconut milk, then into hot oil to make cakes called *kueh lompang* or Swaying Flower Cakes, as they are light enough to flutter in a stiff breeze.

3, 4, 5 Basket molds The "basket" referred to here is actually made of strips of yam, potato, or noodles, arranged in such a way that when deep-fried, they produce little edible bowls that can be used to contain various stir-fried ingredients. The traditional model comprises two large perforated ladles shaped to fit one inside the other. The handles are bamboo or wood, set at a right angle to the bowls. Strips of yam or sweet potato are first dusted with cornstarch or tapioca flour, then laid into the larger ladle to form a kind of nest. The smaller ladle is then used to press down firmly on this nest. The flour acts as a binder and, when deep-fried, these baskets hold their shape firmly. The modern version is much like a pair of wire mesh sieves held together by a hinge. Also available are perforated models without handles. These float freely in the hot oil during cooking. They are more difficult to use because there is nothing to help press the basket ingredients together while in the oil.

making edible baskets

Cut the vegetable strips to be as thin as possible (left) so that they are pliable enough to sit easily in the mold (right). There should be no visible gaps between the strips at the base of the mold. A thorough dusting of cornstarch helps the strips to seal properly. For an attractive brim, leave 1 inch above the top of the mold (bottom). Yam is preferred for its starchy, crisp texture and delicious flavor. Potatoes can also be used. They need to be long enough to yield 4- to 5-inch strips.

shrimp in a yam basket

An impressive dish for dinner parties, this spectacular basket filled with succulent stir-fried shrimp is easier to make than it looks, especially when you have the right tools for the job. Gently swirling the yam basket around in the oil while deep-frying will help it to brown.

Serves 4

Preparation time: 30 minutes

Tools	Ingredients	Method
Yam basket mold	1 large yam, cut into fine strips	**1.** Toss the strips of yam in the cornstarch. Lay them in the lower ladle of mold, overlapping slightly. Press firmly with the upper ladle.
Wok	4 tbsp. cornstarch	
Cleaver	oil for deep-frying	
Cutting board	salad leaves, to garnish	**2.** Heat the oil in the wok and fry the basket until crisp and golden.
	For the filling	**3.** Gently lift the mold out of the oil and pry the yam basket loose. Place it on a serving dish that has been dressed with leaves.
	3 tbsp. oil	
	2 cloves garlic, crushed	
	1 small carrot, cubed	**4.** To make the filling, heat the oil in the cleaned wok and stir-fry the garlic for 1 minute. Add the carrot, celery, and mushrooms and stir-fry for 2 minutes. Add the shrimp, sesame oil, pepper, ginger juice, and oyster sauce, and continue cooking for 5 minutes.
	1 stalk celery, sliced	
	20 button mushrooms	
	1¾ cups jumbo shrimp, shelled with tails left on	
	2 tbsp. sesame oil	
	1 tsp. black pepper	**5.** Blend the cornstarch with a little water and add it to the wok. Stir until the sauce thickens. Transfer to the yam basket and serve.
	1 tbsp. ginger juice	
	2 tbsp. oyster sauce	
	1 tbsp. cornstarch	

top hats

Crispy little cups of feather-light fried batter, these exotic "vol au vents" are unique to Southeast Asia, where they are known as *kueh pietee*. Filled with a savory mixture of jicama and bamboo strips, they make delightful appetizers or finger food for parties.

Makes 40

Preparation time: 1 hour

Tools	Ingredients	Method

Tools
Cleaver
Cutting board
Garlic crusher
Vegetable shredder
Large bowl
Small bowl
Sieve
Small, deep pot
Pietee mold
Small, deep cup
Long chopsticks

Ingredients

For the batter
2½ cups all-purpose flour
2½ cups water
1 tsp. salt
3 eggs
oil for deep-frying

For the filling
7 oz. jicama
14-oz. can bamboo shoots
4 tbsp. oil
4 cloves garlic, crushed
3 tbsp. canned yellow beans
3 tbsp. dark soy sauce
2 cups water
cilantro leaves, to garnish
chili sauce, to serve

Method

1. To make the filling, peel the jicama and cut into fine julienne about 1 inch long. Do the same with the bamboo shoots.

2. Heat the oil in the wok and fry the crushed garlic for 2 minutes. Add the canned yellow beans and mash lightly with the wok ladle. Add the julienned vegetables and stir-fry for 2 minutes. Add the soy sauce and water, bring to a boil over a high heat, and boil for 10 minutes. Reduce the heat to medium and simmer for 20 minutes, or until almost dry.

3. Meanwhile, make the batter. Put the flour in a bowl and make a well in the center. Add the water gradually, mixing into a batter the consistency of pouring cream. Add the salt and stir well.

4. Break the eggs into a separate bowl and beat lightly. Add them to the batter, stirring until well incorporated. Strain through a sieve and chill for 1 hour.

5. Heat the oil for deep-frying in a small saucepan, making sure the depth of oil is greater than the depth of the pietee mold. Place some of the batter in a small, deep cup. When dipped, the base of the mold should not be able to touch the bottom of the pot or the cup, or the batter will smear.

6. When the oil is smoking hot, immerse the mold in it for at least 5 minutes to heat thoroughly. Lift the mold out and gently shake off the excess oil.

7. Dip the mold quickly and, without quivering, into the batter, making sure you do not dip the mold in beyond its rim or the resulting fried cup will be "locked" onto it.

8. Dip the coated mold into the hot oil. Within 1–2 minutes, the batter will turn light brown. When it is golden brown, lift out the mold and gently pry the cup away using chopsticks. Set aside to drain while you cook the remaining cups.

9. To serve, place about 2 tsp. of the warm filling into each cup and garnish with cilantro leaves. Serve with chili sauce.

pots and pans

The wok is the favored pan for everyday cooking in Southeast Asia, but other types of pot are in frequent use, not only for making specialties but also for common dishes such as soups. Pressure cookers speed up cooking of key staples, and in households of Chinese heritage, the steamboat is a popular dish for communal cooking and eating.

1 Pressure cooker This is an indispensable utensil for a number of dishes that require long, slow cooking without the attendant reduction of liquids. Braised belly pork in five-spice powder, beef rendang, and green mung beans in coconut milk, for example, take less than half the normal time to cook when made in a pressure cooker. It also obviates the need for presoaking when cooking foods such as soybeans and black sticky rice.

2 Double-boiler This modern version of the old Chinese utensil is used for slow simmering and stewing. The water boils in the aluminum base, conducting steam to the upper porcelain container. It can be used for custards and other egg mixtures, slow-cooked herbal stews, such as chicken with ginseng, and soups containing delicate ingredients.

3 Electric steamboat Today's electric steamboat is related to the ancient Mongolian firepot used in China and Korea. The modern versions are cleaner and safer to use than the traditional charcoal-fired models but lack rustic appeal. Steamboats are used in several parts of Asia; typical ingredients differ according to available ingredients and favorite local dipping sauces. In Thailand, a spicy tom yam version is produced, whereas the Sichuanese steamboat is flavored with chilies and at one time included poppy heads.

4 Steamboat accessories Brass or aluminum wire mesh individual spoons are specially made for dunking raw foods into the steamboat. Each diner is given one in which to place preferred foods for cooking to a desired consistency or doneness. This prevents portions from floating around and becoming overcooked. When all the food is eaten, the resulting broth is usually very rich from all the different flavors of meat, poultry, seafood, and vegetables that have been cooked.

5, 6 Simmering pots Southeast Asian households have a range of quality pots and saucepans to do jobs that the wok does not do well, such as blanching, making soups and broths, and cooking noodles and congee. Nonstick models are useful to prevent scorching.

steamboat

The last word in tabletop cooking, the steamboat is both a festive meal and a heart-warming way to entertain. The work lies solely in the preparation of raw ingredients. These can be anything you like, as long as they are sliced into bite-sized pieces. A rich broth is made from either chicken bones or bouillon cubes and then transferred to the moat of the steamboat. The stock traditionally is heated by charcoal lit under the moat, but electric models are also available. Diners help themselves to whatever they want and cook their food to suit their tastes.

Serves 10–14
Preparation time: 45 minutes

Tools	Ingredients
Large pot	4 qt. chicken broth
Cleaver	14 oz. lean pork fillet
Cutting board	14 oz. lean beef fillet
Steamboat	14 oz. chicken breast
Wire mesh spoons	2 cups tiger shrimp, peeled
	20 fishballs
	7 oz. pig's liver *(optional)*
	7 oz. squid
	1¾ cups tofu
	4 oz. transparent vermicelli, soaked until soft
	1 Chinese (Napa) cabbage
	light soy sauce, chili sauce, mustard, and pepper, to serve

Method

1. Bring the broth to a boil in a pot. Meanwhile, cut all the ingredients into bite-sized pieces and arrange on presentation plates.

2. Pour the broth in the steamboat, place on the table, and light or switch on. Take the food to the table and set around the steamboat. Provide little dishes of light soy sauce, chili sauce, mustard, and pepper, so the diners can season their cooked food to taste.

3. When the broth begins to bubble, each guest places his or her food of choice into the wire mesh spoons and lays them in the broth to cook.

4. At the end of the meal, the broth will be incredibly rich and can be served as a soup.

beef rendang

This dish moves from boiling to frying in a continuous process, explains writer and cooking teacher Sri Owen, who is the author of several highly regarded works, including *Indonesian Regional Food and Cookery* and *The Rice Book.* "As the water in the coconut milk is driven off, the oil remains, until eventually the meat has absorbed the oil and has become almost black, quite dry but richly succulent, while the solid residue from the oil forms a kind of dry relish." Brisket is the cut of beef Sri recommends for this dish, but bottom round or stew beef are also suitable.

Serves 6–8

Preparation time: 1 hour

Tools	Ingredients	Method
Cleaver	5 shallots	**1.** Peel and finely slice the shallots, and coarsely chop the chilies, garlic, and ginger. Grind them all in the mortar with a pestle.
Cutting board	6 red chilies or 3 tsp. chili powder	**2.** Place all the ingredients in a pressure cooker and cook for about 1 hour.
Mortar and pestle	4 cloves garlic	**3.** Release the pressure by running the cooker under cold running water, then open the lid and stir well. The coconut milk will have turned mostly into oil.
Pressure cooker	1 inch fresh ginger, peeled	**4.** Return the pan to the heat, uncovered, and fry the rendang for about 15 minutes, or until the coconut oil has become thick and brown. Serve with rice.
Ladle	3 lb. 5 oz. beef brisket, cut into ¾-inch strips or cubes	
	1 tsp. ground turmeric	
	1 tsp. chopped galangal or ½ tsp. powdered galangal	
	6 cups coconut milk	
	1 bay leaf	
	1 fresh turmeric leaf or 1 stalk lemongrass	
	2 tsp. salt	

nyonya-style pork curry

Penang, where this dish called "pork gulai" originated, was once the north Malaysian home of the Straits Chinese community known as Babas and Nyonyas. The term *gulai* is Penang patois for any kind of curry or sambal. This recipe comes from neil perry, a leading Australian chef.

Serves 10

Preparation time: 45 minutes

Tools	Ingredients	Method
Cleaver	5 tbsp. coriander seeds	1. In a dry pan, toast the coriander and fennel seeds separately until fragrant, then grind in the mortar.
Cutting board	2 tsp. fennel seeds	2. Peel the squash, cut into large chunks, and steam for 20 minutes until cooked but still firm.
Large pot	3 lb. 5 oz. squash	
Mortar and pestle	2 lb. 12 oz. pork shoulder	3. Meanwhile, cut the pork into bite-sized chunks.
Steamer	10 cloves garlic	Grind the garlic, onion, turmeric, fresh and dried chilies, coriander, and fennel to a paste.
	2 Bermuda onions, minced	
	4 inches fresh turmeric, chopped	4. Heat the oil in a pot. Bruise the lemongrass and fry for 30 seconds before adding the spice paste. Fry over low heat for 4 minutes.
	8 fresh long red chilies, de-seeded, chopped	
	10 dried chilies, soaked in warm water	5. Stir in the coconut cream, star anise, cloves, and cinnamon. Then add the pork, mix well, and cook for about 30 minutes or until the meat is tender.
	⅓ cup oil	
	1 stalk lemongrass	
	1 cup coconut cream	6. Add the steamed squash for the last 5 minutes of cooking, and salt and pepper to taste.
	2 star anise	
	5 cloves	
	1-inch stick cinnamon	
	salt and pepper	

tools for cakes and snacks

In Southeast Asia, cakes and cookies are traditionally associated with symbolism and festive rites, especially during Taoist festivals. Those that originated in China are still held in reverence for their Yin-Yang symbolism. Others evolved from a blend of Indonesian, Malay, and Chinese cultures.

4 Cookie molds This is for small cakes known as *kueh koya*. They are made of mung bean flour and usually feature leaf or fruit motifs. Plastic models are also available.

5 Curry puff mold Curry puffs, the half-moon-shaped Anglo-Indian pasties with crimped edges, were traditionally shaped by hand, but this fold-over plastic mold makes the job easier, neater, and faster.

6 Round cutter Aluminum rings in various sizes are used to stamp out rounds of pastry and dough.

7 Brass crimper and roller This clever double-ended tool is for decorating and shaping crumbly cookies of rice and coconut milk.

8 Melon baller Shown here is a heart-shaped version of a melon baller. In Southeast Asia, melon balls are often served piled up in large fruit shells or are added to sweet drinks. They are sometimes used as a filling for rice and wheat flour cakes, instead of red bean paste.

9 Boat-shaped tart mold Looking like little aluminum boats, these molds are used for the pastry base for pineapple and fruit tarts, usually served during Chinese New Year.

10 Grooved metal tart mold This oval mold contains an inset piece of wood for shaping pastry cases. It stamps each case to give a raised rim. Mashed pineapple is then piled inside for baking.

1, 3 Longevity cake molds Paisley or round templates are carved from wooden blocks and feature motifs symbolic of long life and prosperity.

2 Mooncake mold Mooncakes are made of rice-flour dough and filled with sweet almond or mung bean paste, pressed into the mold, gently tapped out, and steamed or baked. The molds are made of hardwood and carved with designs symbolic of the moon and its role in mythology.

curry puffs

These Malaysian snacks look like small calzone and are usually filled with a curried potato and chicken or lamb mixture. They are believed to have evolved during colonial days when British expatriates and rubber plantation owners, missing their traditional meat pies (pasties), asked their cooks to come up with something similar containing meat and potato. Most cooks in those days were indentured workers from South India, so spices were usually featured heavily in cooking. Malaysia has a nice fusion-style curried pastry or turnover. If you do not wish to make your own dough, use 14 oz. of ready-made basic pastry.

Makes 20

Preparation time: 35 minutes

Tools

Cutting board
Cleaver
Large bowl
Small rolling pin
3-inch cookie cutter
Wok and ladle
Curry puff mold
Wire mesh strainer

Ingredients

For the dough
2⅔ cups all-purpose flour,
   plus extra for dusting
a pinch of salt
4 tbsp. butter or margarine
5 tbsp. water
For the filling
2 tbsp. curry powder
1 tbsp. oil, plus extra for deep-frying
2 cloves garlic, crushed
11 oz. ground lamb
⅔ cup potato, peeled and finely diced
1 tsp. salt
1 tsp. sugar

Method

1. To make the pastry, mix the flour and salt in a bowl and rub in the butter to give a crumbly texture. Add the water and knead well until the dough comes away from the bowl. Roll out the pastry to ⅛ inch thick and cut out circles with the cookie cutter. Set aside.

2. Mix the curry powder with 2 tbsp. water to make a paste. Heat 1 tbsp. oil in the wok, and fry the crushed garlic until light brown. Add the curry paste, and stir over low heat for 4 minutes.

3. Add the meat and potato. Stir until the meat is cooked and the mixture is moist but not watery. Mix in the salt and sugar, then leave to cool.

4. Place a circle of pastry in the curry puff mold and add 1 tbsp. of the meat mixture. Close up and seal the edges to get a half-moon-shaped package, with crimped edges. Repeat with the remaining dough circles.

5. Clean out the wok and heat some oil in it for deep-frying. Cook the curry puffs until golden brown. Drain on paper towels before serving.

longevity cakes

The Chinese name of *ang ku kueh* is translated to mean "red turtle cakes" for two reasons. Red is symbolic of prosperity, and the turtle of longevity. Each mold is usually etched with the design of a turtle or a Chinese character for prosperity, and the cake is dyed red for good measure.

Serves 6
Preparation time: 1 hour, plus overnight soaking

Tools	Ingredients
Cleaver	1 cup diced sweet potato
Cutting board	1¾ cups glutinous rice flour
Saucepans	1¼ cups coconut milk
Colander	3 tbsp. sugar
Mixing bowl	a pinch of salt
Steamer	½ tsp. cochineal red coloring
Longevity cake molds	*For the filling*
Banana leaves	2 cups shelled mung beans, soaked overnight
	1 cup water
	2 cups sugar

Method

1. In a small pan, simmer the sweet potato in water to cover for 5 minutes, then drain and mash well with a fork. Mix with half the glutinous rice flour, half the coconut milk, and the sugar and salt.

2. Bring the remaining coconut milk to a slow simmer and mix with the rest of the glutinous rice flour. Stir well to make a thick dough.

3. Combine both doughs and knead on a floured board for 5 minutes. Add the coloring and knead to incorporate thoroughly.

4. To make the filling, drain the soaked beans into a steamer tray and cook for 15 minutes or until very soft. Mash well.

5. Place the water and sugar in a pan and boil to make a thick syrup. Add the mashed beans and cook over a low heat until the mixture is very dry and thick. Set aside to cool.

6. Oil the palms of your hands and divide the dough into lemon-sized balls. Flatten a little, then make a deep dent in the center of the dough and fill with 1 tbsp. of the bean filling (top left). Close up and seal.

7. Press the filled ball into a mold (center) and apply gentle pressure so that the design of the mold is deeply etched on the surface of the cake when turned out (below).

8. Soak the banana leaves in hot water and cut into squares slightly larger than the cakes. Place a cake on each square, put in the steamer, and cook for 15 minutes. Serve cold.

tools for cakes and snacks

Some of the most distinctive candies of Southeast Asia have transcended their festive and symbolic roles to become everyday snacks sold by street hawkers, restaurants, and gourmet retailers. Such is their popularity that traditional molds have been given the high-tech treatment. Once in danger of becoming extinct, these now hold a high place in the region's culinary cultures.

1, 2 Kueh bolu molds These molds are used for little egg-based sponge cakes known as *kueh bolu*. The traditional model is brass or copper, with a lid designed to contain hot charcoal on top, whereas the mold itself is heated in a clay oven. The modern version is much the same but runs on electricity. The molds are shaped with floral and animal motifs symbolic of luck or prosperity, or simply to look pretty for festive occasions.

3, 4 Love letter molds *Kueh blander*, or love letters, are traditional egg rolls, wafer-thin and crisp, that originated in China but are now made mainly in Southeast Asia. The molds were made of iron and featured two plates etched with heraldic designs clasped tightly together and attached to long handles for manipulating over a charcoal brazier. The modern electric version looks like a waffle maker. The word *blander* refers to a species of crab that mates for life and are always found in pairs in the coastal areas of Malaysia. The belief is that the cakes were originally made to hide secret messages between lovers and warring factions.

little sponge cakes

The name of these charming festive cakes, *kueh bolu*, literally means "round cakes," not because of their shape but in homage to the moon. Once reserved for Chinese New Year, *kueh bolu* are now eaten all year round, thanks to the ease with which they can be made in modern electric molds. These cakes are easy to produce, but for best results it is essential to beat the eggs with an electric whisk until the mixture is white and frothy.

Serves 4
Preparation time: 40 minutes

Tools	Ingredients
Large bowl	6 eggs
Electric whisk	⅔ cup sugar
Mortar and pestle	½ cup all-purpose flour
Electric kueh bolu mold	a pinch of salt
Pastry brush	4 tbsp. coconut milk
Chopsticks	2 pandanus leaves

Method

1. Crack the eggs into a large bowl. Add the sugar and salt and beat with an electric whisk until the mixture is white and frothy.
2. Stir in the flour and coconut milk and blend to give a smooth batter.
3. Grind the pandanus leaves with the pestle to extract the liquid essence, then strain this into the egg mixture.
4. Heat the kueh bolu machine and thoroughly oil each mold with a pastry brush. Pour a little batter into each mold to fill to just below the rim (top picture) because the cakes will swell a little when cooked.
5. Clamp down the lid and cook until the cakes are light brown, about 3 minutes. Allow to cool before removing from the machine with a pair of chopsticks (bottom picture). The little cakes will keep for a few weeks in an airtight container.

serving items

Meals throughout Southeast Asia are communal, served simply on banana leaves and in ordinary plates and bowls. For special occasions such as weddings and birthdays, however, presentation becomes spectacular, with gloriously colorful bamboo baskets to hold bulky items. The preserved fruits and candies traditionally served at Chinese New Year and Taoist festivals are presented in smaller decorated baskets, often exquisitely crafted to please the various deities.

1 Painted baskets Traditional painted baskets of woven bamboo called *sia na* were used for wedding gifts in earlier times. Some of these could be large enough to hold bottles of wine, syrups, whole suckling pigs, fruits, and so on. Smaller ones were used for cakes and candy carried by members of the groom's family to the bride's home on the important day, to sweeten their thoughts and lives. Much of this craft is now dying out, but with ingenuity, the same designs have been molded in porcelain for the same functions. Some baskets are single-tiered, others are stacked in twos and threes. They make ideal serving utensils for snacks and side dishes such as shrimp crackers, fried shallots, peanut wafers, and other tidbits.

2 Porcelain banana leaf rice plate Banana leaves were traditionally used as disposable plates throughout Southeast Asia. Rural Indonesians and Malays still eat from leaves and other natural containers, and in urban areas, banana leaves are still very much associated with meal presentation. They are often used to line serving and dining plates, especially for festive and other special occasion dishes. They bring a colorfully rustic touch to any Southeast Asian meal and are used in southern India, too. Today, you can also find these porcelain versions in good tableware outlets.

3 Lacquered stacking basket Throughout Southeast Asia, basketry remains a fundamental element in the home. Not only do these baskets serve a purpose, but they are also often fine *objets d'art*, like this multitiered model for sweets and candies for festive occasions.

Flatware (*not shown*) The standard place setting for most Southeast Asian meals served with rice would be a dinner plate, fork, and spoon, the flatware usually being made of stainless steel or local materials such as horn or brass. To the surprise of many non-Asians, chopsticks are not much used in this region except when noodles are served. The knife, as used in the West, never appears on Asian tables because it is considered a chef's tool, and too barbaric to be used at the table. Nor does it serve any purpose in traditional meals, because no Asian dish requires food to be cut up at the table—all ingredients are cut into bite-sized pieces during preparation. If soup is served during a meal, whether it is presented in individual bowls or in a large bowl placed at the center of the table, a porcelain spoon and rest will be provided.

nasi lemak with hot chili sambal, wok-fried eggs, whitebait, and peanuts

Nasi lemak began as a hawker dish many decades ago, when a simple portion of coconut rice would be wrapped in a banana leaf and flavored with a thick, hot sambal. Today it is a veritable smorgasbord of delicious proportions and may include a curry, pickles, shrimp crackers, an omelet, and fried fish, as well as the sambal. Together, the result is more than the sum of its parts and is typically served for breakfast. Below is a recipe for coconut rice and a few classic accompaniments. The whitebait used is not fresh, but rather a dried product called *ikan billis* that is sold in most Chinese and Southeast Asian stores. The fried tamarind-marinated mackerel (opposite) can be included as part of the meal. Alternatively, you could serve a beef stew or chicken curry.

coconut rice
Wash 1¾ cups jasmine rice and soak in water for 30 minutes. Drain and place on a steamer tray. Wash and tie 2 pandanus leaves into knots and press them down into the rice. Add 1¾ cups coconut milk and 1 tsp. salt, and mix well. Place in a steamer and cook for 15 minutes. To serve, place the rice on a banana leaf–covered plate and top with a wok-fried egg and a little sambal. Serve some sliced cucumber and other side dishes in baskets or small plates.

hot chili sambal
In a mortar, grind 1 large onion, 3 cloves garlic, 4 fresh red chilies, and 2 tsp. shrimp paste. Heat 4 tbsp. oil in a wok and fry the paste over low heat until fragrant. Add 1 tbsp. tomato paste, 2 tbsp. tamarind sauce, 1 tsp. salt, 1 tsp. sugar, and continue cooking 1 minute. When the mixture thickens, remove to a bowl to cool.

wok-fried eggs
Place 4 eggs in a saucepan of cold water, bring to a boil, and simmer for 6 minutes. Drain and cool under cold running water, then shell the eggs. In a clean wok, heat 1 tbsp. oil, add the eggs, and roll them around the pan until a brown skin forms. Cut in half before serving, topped with the sambal if desired.

fried whitebait and peanuts
Shake off any excess grit from 1 cup dried whitebait or ikan bilis. Heat 3 tbsp. oil in a wok and stir-fry the whitebait for 4 minutes until brown and crisp. Remove from the wok and set aside. Add 1 cup shelled, skinned peanuts to the wok, toss to brown lightly and serve alongside, or mixed with, the fish.

fried tamarind-marinated mackerel

A faithful companion to coconut rice, these mackerel pieces are first steeped in tamarind paste, drained, and fried until crisp, to produce a dish known as *ikan goreng asam*. The sweet flesh of the mackerel takes on a special flavor when served with hot chili sambal. Like any food with a tamarind coating, the fish will turn dark brown when fried.

Serves 4

Preparation time: 25 minutes

Tools	Ingredients
Cleaver	1 large mackerel, about 1 lb. 5 oz.
Cutting board	2 tbsp. tamarind paste
Mixing bowl	⅔ cup water
Wok and ladle	1 tbsp. light soy sauce
Draining rack	oil for deep-frying

Method

1. Cut the mackerel into four thick steaks, discarding the head and tail fin.
2. In a bowl, blend the tamarind paste with the water and soy sauce, add the fish, and marinate for 10 minutes.
3. Heat some oil for deep-frying in a wok. Drain the fish and pat dry with a paper towel.
4. Deep fry the fish for about 4 minutes, turning once during cooking.
5. Drain on the rack, then serve alone with sambal, or as a part of a *nasi lemak* meal.

coconut egg jam

The importing of European preserves into Southeast Asia during colonial times must have triggered the desire for sweet spreads on bread. Given that coconuts abound in the region, it was only a matter of time before this delicious coconut and egg jam was born. Called *kaya* in the Malay language, its incredible richness best explains the name, which means "rich," as in "wealthy."

Serves 10

Preparation time: 3 hours

Tools	Ingredients
2 large bowls	20 eggs
Chopsticks	3 cups coconut milk
Fine sieve	2 cups sugar
Double boiler	4 pandanus leaves, tied into knots
Ladle	

Method

1. Crack the eggs into a bowl and beat lightly with chopsticks. Strain through a fine sieve into another clean bowl, then strain a second time.
2. Add the coconut milk and sugar and stir gently for 30 minutes, until the sugar has almost dissolved.
3. Transfer the mixture to the double boiler and fill the bottom container two-thirds full with water. Cover and bring to a boil.
4. Using the ladle, stir the mixture slowly but continuously for 15 minutes. Rest for 15 minutes, stir for 15 minutes, then rest again, and continue this pattern until the mixture is thick and glossy, about 2 hours. Halfway through cooking, add the pandanus leaves.
5. Transfer the kaya to a bowl and leave to cool. Cover and store in a sealed jar. Serve with toast or bread.

suppliers

The following list incorporates sources of the equipment featured in the photographs in this book, as well as other useful suppliers of Asian kitchenware and ingredients including retailers, importers, markets, and wholesalers.

united states

Gumps
135 Post Street
San Francisco, California 94108
Tel: 800 766 7628
www.gumps.com

Joyce Chen Asian Cookware
20 University Boulevard
East Silver Spring, Maryland 20901
Tel: 201 593 8905

Asia Cook
Suite 30, 2850 Ocean Park Boulevard
Santa Monica, California 90405
Tel: 310 450 3270
www.asia4sale.com

Mrs. Lin's Kitchen
2415 San Ramon Valley Boulevard
San Ramon, California 94583-4743
Tel: 925 830 9053
e-mail: custsvl@mrslinskitchen.com

Williams Sonoma
150 Post Street
San Francisco, California 94108
Tel: 415 362 6904
www.williams-sonoma.com

Pottery Barn
2390 Market Street
San Francisco, California 94114
Tel: 415 861 0800
www.potterybarn.com

Crate and Barrel
Direct Marketing
1860 West Jefferson Avenue
Naperville, Illinois 60540
Tel: 630 579 9000
www.crateandbarrel.com

Spice Merchant
P.O. Box 524
1035 Longhorn Drive
Jackson, Wyoming 83001
Tel: 307 551 5999
e-mail: stirfry@compuserve.com

Fax Run Craftsmen
P.O. Box 72, 1907 Stout Drive
Ivyland, PA 18974
Tel: 215 675 7700

House of Spices
127–40 Willets Point Blvd
Flushing, New York 11368-1506
Tel: 718 507 4600
e-mail: hosindia@aol.com

India Foods & Spices
80 River Street
Cambridge, Massachusetts 02139-3805
Tel: 617 497 6144

The British Express
2880 SW 42nd Avenue
Palm City, Florida 34990
Tel: 888 840 1280 and 561 219 0664

Dean and Deluca
560 Broadway
New York, New York 10012
Tel: 212 226 6800
www.deandeluca.com

Zabar's
2245 Broadway
New York, New York 10024
Tel: 212 496 1234
www.zabars.com

Sunrise Mart
4 Stuyvesant Street, 2nd Floor
New York, New York 10003
Tel: 212 598 3040

Katagiri
224 and 244 East 59th Street
New York, New York 10022
Tel: 212 755 3566

Pearl River Mart
277 Canal Street
New York, New York 10013
Tel: 800 878 2446
www.pearlriver.com

Bridge Kitchenware
214 East 52nd Street
New York, New York 10022
Tel: 212 688 4220
www.bridgekitchenware.com

Broadway Panhandler
477 Broome Street
New York, New York 10013
Tel: 212 966 3434
www.broadwaypanhandler.com

Global Table
109 Sullivan Street
New York, New York 10012
Tel: 212 431 5839

Spice Corner
135 Lexington Avenue
New York, New York 10016
Tel: 212 689 5128

canada

Annapurna Mithai Shoppe
1544 Warden Avenue
Scarborough, Ontario M1R 2S8
Tel: 416 449 0157

Dino's Grocery Mart
460 Notre Dame Avenue
Winnipeg, Manitoba R3V 1R5
Tel: 204 942 1526

IndianLife Food Corporation
3835 2nd Avenue
Burnaby, British Columbia V5C 3W7
Tel: 604 205 9176
www.indianlife.com

Fox Run Craftsmen
Unit 1, 535 Millway Avenue
Concord, Ontario L4K 3V4
Tel: 905 669 4145

asia

Lau Choy Seng
23–25 Temple Street
Singapore
Tel: 065 6223 5486
e-mail: sales@lauchoyseng.com
e-mail: lcspl@singnet.com.sg

Rishi Handicrafts
58 Arab Street
Singapore
Tel: 065 6298 5927 and 065 6298 2408

Tang's Department Store
310–320 Orchard Road
Singapore
Tel: 065 6737 5500
www.tangs.com

Yue Hwa Chinese Emporium
70 Eu Tong Sen Street
Singapore
Tel: 065 6538 4222

Sia Huat
Retail Sales
7–11 Temple Street
Singapore 058559
Tel: 065 6223 1732
e-mail: enquiry@siahuat.com.sg
www.siahuat.com.sg

Sia Huat
Head Office
20 Pandan Road
Singapore 609272
Tel: 0065 6268 3922

Hocatsu (M) Sdn Bhd
6 Jalan SS, 21/35 Damansara Utama,
Petaling Jaya, Selangor Darul Ehsan
Tel: 00603 7725 4588
e-mail: hocatsu@pd.jaring.my

PT Hocatsu Pratama
Ruko Marina Mangga Dua Block C
7–8 Jalan Gunung Sahan Raya, No 2
Jakarta
Tel: 006221 640 4777
e-mail: sales@hocatsu-pratama.com
www.hocatsu-pratama.com

Central Plaza
1693 Phahonyothin Road
Lardprao, Chatuchak, Bangkok 10900
Tel: 662 937 1555
e-mail: property@centralgroup.com

Chatuchak Weekend Market
Off Phahonyothin Road,
across from Mo Chit Bus Terminal

united kingdom

Oriental City Supermarket
399 Edgware Road
Colindale, London NW9
Tel: 020 8200 0009
e-mail: phoebe@oriental-city.com
www.oriental-city.com

Typhoon Europe Ltd
Oakcroft Road
Chessington, Surrey
Tel: 0208 974 4750
e-mail: info@typhooneurope.com
www.typhooneurope.com

Imperial International
Sheene Road
Beaumont Leys, Leicester
Tel: 0116 291 9999
www.imperialint.com

useful web sites

www.deliciousindia.com
www.ethnicgrocer.com
www.namaste.com
www.indiandelicacies.com

index

numbers in italics refer to the ingredient
identification pictures in chapter introductions

bibliography

Andoh, Elizabeth, *At Home with Japanese Cooking* (Knopf, 1980)
Booth, Shirley, *Food of Japan* (Grub Street, 2000)
Davidson, Alan, *Seafood of South East Asia* (Federal Publications, 1976)
Dunlop, Fuchsia, *Sichuan Cookery* (Michael Joseph, 2001)
Gordon, Peter, *Cook at Home with Peter Gordon* (Hodder and Stoughton, 1999)
Hsiung, Deh-ta, *The Chinese Kitchen* (Kyle Cathie, 2001)
Kazuko, Emi, *Street Café Japan* (Conran Octopus, 1999)
Owen, Sri, *Indonesian Regional Food and Cookery* (Frances Lincoln, 1999)
Panjabi, Camellia, *50 Great Curries of India* (Kyle Cathie, 2000)
Simonds, Nina, *Asian Noodles* (Hearst Books, 1997)
Sreedharan, Das, *New Tastes of India* (Headline, 2001)
Thompson, David, *Thai Food* (Pavilion, 2003)
Todiwala, Cyrus, *Café Spice Namaste* (Ebury Press, 1998)
Tsai, Ming, *Blue Ginger* (Pavilion Books, 2000)

acknowledgments

AUTHOR: As a believer in karma, I would like to mention the propitious telephone call from literary agent Teresa Chris, who asked if I knew anyone who could write a book on Asian cooking tools. Without any false modesty, I said I could do it myself and so it came to pass that I met up with Jacqui Small, to whom I give my most heartfelt thanks for offering me the commission.

Most of all, I would like to thank my editor, Jenni Muir, for her inexhaustible patience, unstinting help in sourcing for guest chefs, and remarkable skill in making sense of my often convoluted copy. To art director Valerie Fong for her invaluable, brilliant artistic and cultural input, unflagging energy, and logistical help throughout the hectic weeks of photography. They are simply the best professionals I have ever worked with and definitely on the A-list of my foodie guests.

I am also indebted to Tym and Tony Yeoh for their help in sourcing rare Indo-Chinese tools and their contribution of information on Thai culinary heritage. To all my family members who turned their kitchens inside out for family-owned tools. To photographers Michael Paul and Nat Rea for their inspiring work in capturing the true essence of the food and tools.

Thanks also to my friends and fellow chefs, and the Blue Elephant Group in the U.K. for their guest contributions, to the chefs of the Raffles, Furama, and Shangri-La Hotels in Singapore, and all the chefs from the global front. Special thanks to Oriental City Supermarket, Colindale, Typhoon Europe Ltd., and Yoshikin (U.K.) for the loan of their items.

PUBLISHER: Thanks to Emi Kazuko and Roopa Gulati for help with photography, sourcing equipment, and advice on culinary matters in their specialties. Thanks also to Betty Fong.

We would like to thank the following for contributing recipes to this book (in order of appearance): Fuchsia Dunlop, Peter Tsang, Deh-ta Hsiung, Ming Tsai, Shirley Booth, Emi Kazuko, Roy Yamaguchi, Peter Gordon, Elizabeth Andoh, Das Sreedharan, Cyrus Todiwala, Menernosh Mody, Yogesh Arora, Camellia Panjabi, Chef Chang, David Thompson, Marlena Spieler, Alan Davidson, Hong Sai Choi, Sri Owen, and Neil Perry. All guest recipes are used with permission.